COVENTRY LIBRARIES

Please return this book on or before
the last date stamped below.

To renew this book take it to any of
the City Libraries before
the date due for return

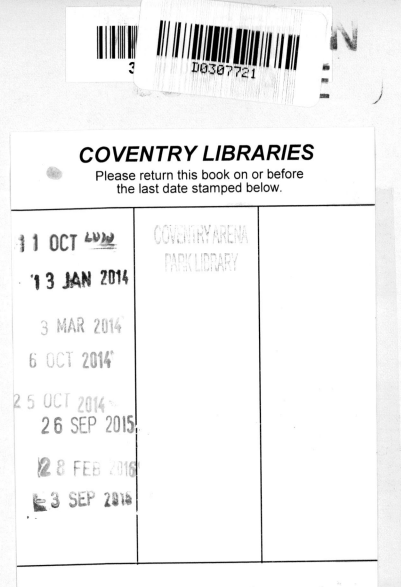

Coventry City Council

It Could Happen to You

The Inspirational Story of the Crime Victim Who Became the People's Crusader

HELEN NEWLOVE

MAINSTREAM
PUBLISHING

EDINBURGH AND LONDON

Copyright © Helen Newlove 2013

All rights reserved

The moral right of the author has been asserted

First published in Great Britain in 2013 by

MAINSTREAM PUBLISHING COMPANY

(EDINBURGH) LTD

7 Albany Street

Edinburgh EH1 3UG

ISBN 9781780575858

A catalogue record for this book is available from the British Library

Printed in Great Britain by
CPI Group (UK) Ltd, Croydon, CR0 4YY

1 3 5 7 9 10 8 6 4 2

This is for my daughters, my wonderful girls who have grown up strong and true, gifted and beautiful women inside and out. They have had to grow up fast, always shadowed by our tragedy, which thrust all of us into the limelight we would have preferred to avoid.

Acknowledgements

Writing this book is one of the hardest things I have ever had to do. Recalling the happy times and reliving the darkest days has been a rollercoaster of emotions, and often tears streamed down my face as the words poured out. I had bottled it up for so long. It made me open doors in my heart and mind I would have preferred to leave tightly closed, so painful has been the journey.

It's a chance to put my side of the story, of my journey. We have to stand up for decency, for the right way to live with our neighbours, and to fearlessly tackle the violent elements that threaten our happiness. And it is an opportunity to tell Garry's story so the grandchildren he will never see or hold will know what an amazing man he was, and be proud of him as we all are.

This thank-you list will be a long one, but I want to thank my daughters Zoe, Danielle and Amy from the bottom of my heart. Only they truly know what this journey has been like, and how it has affected us all. I'm honoured and humbled that they have allowed me to share our experiences, good and bad. I want to thank my loving parents who have been there for me; my sister and brother-in-law; Garry's brother, sister and nephews; my dearest friends Tina and Gary; and all those who have given me the strength to battle on for changes in society to prevent others losing their lives in such a senseless, cruel and violent way.

I am very proud and honoured to have Warrington as part of my title, and I'd like to thank the community in Fearnhead, and the whole of the town, for their love and support during our darkest moments. The people of Warrington stood shoulder-to-shoulder with us in the days and weeks after Garry's murder, and we will never forget that. Special thanks go to Canon Stephen Attwater, who presided over Garry's funeral and the memorial service a year later.

The Warrington Wolves Foundation helped the Newlove family to find the will to go and do something positive for the town. With their help, we set up NewloveWarrington, of which I'm immensely proud. I'd like to thank Wolves Foundation Trustee John Gartside, as well as Wolves owner Simon Moran and comedian Peter Kay for their help in organising the gala night that brought NewloveWarrington into being.

The media doesn't get much thanks these days, but I will pay tribute to those journalists who brought the news of Garry's death to the nation, reporting the facts carefully and respecting our privacy. The police are often in the firing line too, but I can't thank Cheshire Police enough for their total support and dedication to duty throughout.

I would like to thank Rani King for her work bringing this book to fruition, and to my agent, editor, book logo artist Jeni McConnell and all at Mainstream who enabled me to reach out and be heard. I'm pleased to say that profits from this book will be donated to charities working with victims of crime and vulnerable members of the community.

To my political friends David Cameron, Eric Pickles, my noble friends in the House of Lords and those in the Commons from all parties, and the great British public, whose affection and support for us has kept us going, I send this simple message:

you listened, you shared our grief and outrage, and helped this Northern lass take on the establishment and speak up for victims everywhere. There are few words to express my gratitude. Watch this space – I'm not done yet . . .

Finally, for Paul, who taught me to love, laugh and live again. And that there are rainbows after the heaviest shower, and stars in the darkest of nights if you have faith and never give up looking for them.

Contents

ONE

Early Days

Salford in the early 1960s hadn't changed much since its industrial heyday at the turn of the century. Grubby kids still played outside rows of flat-fronted terraced houses while housewives gossiped over yard walls. Many, if not most, people worked in the mills whose chimneys loomed large over the whole area. It was a poor, damp and dirty environment, not made any better by the fact that the cotton industry was in decline, but it was very neighbourly. People cared for and respected one another. I can remember 'pea-soupers', when the fog mixed with all the soot to make an evil-smelling, greenish-grey smog that hung around in the atmosphere. You could not see your hand in front of your face. We had to walk with our hands in front of us so we would not bump into walls. Cars would have to drive very slowly with their hazard lights on full in the daytime. It was so dangerous. The damp affected people's health, and bronchitis and pneumonia were commonplace. On a crisp winter's morning with ice sparkling and when the air was clear, it looked and felt like being in an L.S. Lowry painting. It was very picturesque, but not at all pleasant.

In the summer, it got so hot that we all kept our doors open as we sat on the polished steps, which sparkled in the sunshine.

They were the pride and joy of our homes. If your house had a perfectly scrubbed doorstep, it meant you were respectable. During summertime, there was little breeze and the tarmac would melt and us kids would use wooden lolly sticks to pick it up and make swirly patterns. All the kids were out 'early doors' and able to walk freely to the park or up and down our streets, playing hopscotch and jumping up and down to silly rhymes with skipping ropes. The boys would get a clip round the ear if they kicked their footballs too close to Mrs Smith's windows or the corner shops. Our Northern version of 'knockdown ginger' was doorman's knock. Some of the kids would creep up, ring the doorbell and then run away laughing while some poor neighbour would rush out into the street telling them off and shaking her fist. Childhood always paints the past with a rose-tinted brush, so I didn't really see the poverty and hardship at the time, but perhaps this brought people closer together. Although it's classed as a city, Salford then seemed much more like a village, with a tight-knit community and traditional family values. Those values in a world that was changing quickly were captured by scriptwriter Tony Warren, who gave the world his version of the Salford I grew up in: *Coronation Street*.

I was born in December 1961, just a year after the first episode of *Corrie* was screened. My parents, Rose and Terence Marston, were both locals: Mum's family came from Wythenshawe, while Dad is a Salfordian through and through. They met at a church dance, and married and had two daughters: me and my sister, Marie. Both my parents are Roman Catholic and this was the faith I was brought up in. They were strict about it: we never missed Mass on a Sunday and we had to attend on Saints' Days and during school time. We certainly weren't unusual, though, as Salford and Manchester had a huge Roman Catholic population.

My mum was raised by nuns and for a time worked as a

housekeeper to priests. She'd had a hard start to her life. Her father was a merchant seaman and was away at sea a lot, leaving her mother, my nana, to raise four children on her own, and hold down a full-time job. They were very poor and there was no childcare then, the eldest child being the one who helped to look after their younger siblings. My young aunty Bridie died in a terrible accident while Nana was out working. Nana couldn't forgive herself or Granddad, and that was the start of the end. She blamed herself and him and, as she couldn't cope with the grief and the guilt, she left. Mum was only ten at the time and had to leave school to look after her three-year-old sister, Kathleen, and her brother John, who was only fourteen months old. I have such admiration for my mum. Neighbours chipped in to help feed the hungry children, while another paid Mum a shilling a week to scrub her doorstep so they could survive. Mum describes dealing with the rent man and the coalman while their debts mounted up. Granddad was on and off the scene – but mostly off – leaving Mum to keep this chaos going. This went on for a long time until the little family came to the attention of a visiting nun. Luckily, it was decided by Mum's godparents, John and Betty Bowles, that it was in the children's best interests that the Church look after them. Granddad was at sea and couldn't be contacted. So Mum and Kath were sent to Nazareth House in Crosby, near Liverpool, to be raised by the Sisters of Nazareth. Their baby brother, John, was placed in a council home as the convent did not take boys, and Mum didn't set eyes on him again until he was nine years old.

Now, the nuns were strict and there was iron discipline. Punishment was routine and legs were sometimes slapped. But Mum loved it and, to this day, she keeps in touch with some of the nuns who looked after her. Aunty Kath, on the other hand, was a bit of a rebel and used to climb the convent wall to escape. She was always the joker, whereas Mum was the quiet one. As

Mum grew up, she befriended some of the nuns, and when they moved to Oxford she went with them as their housekeeper. By a remarkable coincidence, it was here that she became reunited with her mother. A visiting priest, Father Leonard, remarked on how much my mum reminded him of his cousin who had come from Ireland to marry an Englishman. On questioning, it turned out to be my nana. Mum was 21 then and agreed to meet her. They fell sobbing into each other's arms at the train station, all hurt and separation forgotten. They kept in touch, and eventually Mum moved back to the north-west to be with the new family (her brother John was now living with their mum) and then her sister Kath joined them, so at last they were reunited.

I find it amazing, and a tribute to Mum's character, that she never had any ill feeling towards my nana. In fact, she adored her. After Nana had left, she'd gone on to have three boys, Ray, George and Will, with another man, George Smith, who was my surrogate granddad and whom I loved very much. Mum also adored her three little brothers. She never judged her mum or made an issue of this, which was unusual in those times.

Mum got a job keeping house for two priests in Salford but visited her mum every week on her day off. When Nana got old, Mum willingly looked after her until her dying day. Mum was the sort of person who would get on two buses with her kids to make sure Nana was OK, and frequently did. Nana was a hell of a character and would put aside a bit of her pension for the small weekly bottle of whisky that she loved. I adored her as much as Mum did and was delighted when she eventually came to live with us. She was a very independent woman, though, so it wasn't long before she moved out into sheltered accommodation. Even then, she wouldn't socialise with the other residents – 'Oh, because they're all too old!' she'd shout whenever we asked why she wouldn't sit in the communal lounge. Right up to her death, she was out cleaning her windows at 6 a.m. She always said that if she couldn't walk and talk, she didn't want to be looked after and, finally having suffered a stroke, she was as good as her word. Mum was devastated when she died and so was I. Despite what had happened in Nana's life, she was good fun and I always felt comfortable around her.

Dad's upbringing was also hard. His dad died when he was young and Nana Marston, Dad's mother, was a tough woman. You didn't cross her, and even when she sent Dad to the shop to buy her a quarter of treacle toffee, she would weigh it herself to make sure he hadn't pinched any! Dad was the youngest of five and he was made to do everything at home. Although he loved his mum, he found her regime very tough, and towards the end of the Second World War he deliberately lied about his age to join the Royal Marines. He was accepted and went off to train, but when Nana Marston found out she moved heaven and earth to get him back, telling the authorities he was needed at home. She was successful, but when she eventually did get him back she discovered his time in the Marines hadn't been without incident. A rifle butt had struck Dad in the face during training, causing him to lose a lot of teeth, and he had to wear dentures from that moment on.

Dad never went back into the military, but he always says he would have loved to stay in. It left a lasting legacy. He is still a clean and tidy person, which may well have come from his short time in the Marines. He's the perfect gentleman, very polite towards women and rarely touches alcohol. When he was young, he saw his brothers get into terrible alcohol-fuelled fights and he swore then that he wouldn't be a drinker. He's not much of a social mixer and likes keeping himself to himself. They say opposites attract, so my mum, with her jolly Mancunian and Scouse background and good sense of humour, was perfect for him. In a way, it was the same when I met my husband, Garry: he was the extrovert, while I was the quiet one. Mum and Dad met in Salford at the local Catholic church and have been married for nearly 60 years now. Nana Marston didn't make it easy for them at first, but Mum and Dad got through all that and they've been – and remain – a very solid couple.

I used to love looking at their black and white wedding photos. Mum was dressed in an elegant, smart day dress. In those days, you did not always have a white wedding dress, as money was very tight and you had to get full use out of clothes. Dad had his best suit on and a carnation buttonhole, while Mum carried a small bouquet.

It wasn't easy for Mum to have children and, after her unconventional family history, she was desperate to have a family to cherish, so we were eagerly anticipated and dearly loved. Their first child was my sister, Marie, and I came along five years later. From the time I opened my eyes, I was a poorly child, suffering badly from chest complaints. I was in hospital almost every year for the first few years of my life and I always seemed to be coughing: 'a spring cough', my mum would say, or 'an autumn cough'. The soot-filled air around Salford back then wasn't what you'd describe as healthy, and lots of kids coughed and spluttered, but I seemed to get it worse than anyone else. Finally, a 'spring cough' came that went on into summer and refused to clear up. Mum had already been backwards and forwards to several doctors but hadn't had any joy. When she saw I was going blue in the face, she decided enough was enough and I was taken to the local hospital. The doctor on call who examined me became very concerned when he discovered that the nasty cough was being caused by a hole in my lung, which had been there from birth. I was admitted as an emergency and an Indian doctor sat by my bedside all night. I was only two years old and it was far from certain whether I'd survive, but I pulled through to fight another day.

At about the same age, I had to start wearing glasses because I had a lazy eye which turned in. I had countless eye operations, which were, by today's standards, barbaric. Before the operation, your eyelashes were burned away using a candle and your eyebrows shaved off. In those days, there was no such thing as parents staying overnight with you, so there I was, alone in the confines of Salford's Victorian Hope Hospital (now Salford Royal), wishing my mum and dad would come and dreading the moment when I would be anaesthetised. I still have an absolute horror of hospitals in general and oxygen masks in particular. Finally, when I was 12, I had a successful operation and was told by the doctor that I didn't need to wear glasses again. I just burst into tears. My mum was amazed at my reaction, as was the doctor, who said that it was a first for him. I cried because I had worn glasses for so long that I felt I would look stupid without them.

By that time, we'd moved from Salford. As I said, it was a friendly place to grow up, and even as a toddler I played out in the street with all the other kids. However, it wasn't the place for a child with a bad chest. After my near brush with death, my parents were told they should consider living somewhere cleaner for the sake of my health. Sweden was actually suggested, but apparently my mum refused to leave family behind, so instead of pine forests and tranquil lakes we made the six-mile journey across Salford to Irlam. It was much leafier and greener than Salford, even if it did have a huge steelworks on its doorstep. We moved to a Victorian semi-detached in Clarendon Road. There were only six houses in the row, with council offices and an old fire station opposite, plus a Catholic primary school, St Teresa's, and a huge field at the end of the road. I could almost fall out of bed and into school. Today, there are modern houses where the council offices were, but aside from that the area looks very much the same as it did when I was a child.

Mum was so excited to be in the house. There was a lot to do to it, but she loved every minute of turning it into a home. I remember having a pantry in the kitchen and a clothes pulley on the ceiling, which we hung wet clothes on to dry. I felt dead posh, as we had two big sitting rooms and a bathroom and toilet inside our home instead of having to go outside to the toilet. The bedrooms were huge, and my sister and I had a room each. I had the warmest one because of my chest and it was very snug in the winter. I loved reading and drawing. I played teacher with my dolls and was very happy with my family life. My parents strived to give both my sister and me the best possible upbringing.

Irlam is the place I remember most from my childhood. I was so happy to be there. It seemed a big house to me, with high ceilings, lots of nooks and crannies, and even a cellar. My parents didn't have much money, so they did it up as they went along. Mum was a cook, working in the canteen of a motor-component maker's in Manchester. My dad worked there too, as a packer and supervisor. One year, Mum got very lucky and she won a share of the pools, about £1,200 in all, which was a tidy sum in those days. I knew something had changed, as all of a sudden Mum and Dad started changing the look of the house downstairs. They bought a brand-new central-heating system, which turned the draughty old house into a warm and cosy home. We also had the pantry modernised, which particularly pleased Mum because she loved to cook at home and keep the kitchen spotless. Mum ended up cooking and making butties in our living room as the work was being carried out. We were all scuttling to get around the one and only fireplace in the middle room, as everywhere else was being plumbed in.

Despite all the DIY that he put into the house, Dad never really settled in Irlam. Mind you, he was content in his own company. He was always keen on cars, and if he wasn't tinkering under the bonnet of a Ford or an Austin, he was weeding the garden and digging in plants and vegetables. He was happy that way, whereas my mum got to know the neighbours quickly and soon had lots of friends.

Every year we'd go for a week to Blackpool, staying at the same place with the same people, which gave the holiday a family atmosphere. Every other year we'd go for two weeks, perhaps because my parents needed that time to save up the money.

Dad didn't have much interest in going further than Blackpool, but Mum was more adventurous. The neighbours three doors down, Ann and Bill, were Irish, and Ann became my mum's best friend. We called her Aunty Ann. Her father owned a farm in County Mayo, and when his wife died Aunty Ann left Irlam to look after him. Mum was devastated, but she was determined not to lose contact, and eventually we were invited over for a holiday. Dad didn't want to go, so Mum took me instead. It felt like a hell of a journey then, and I was fascinated by how different Ireland was from England. We went into a local shop and discovered that as well as selling vegetables it also had a little bar that served the local farmers with their daily pints of Guinness. I thought this was amazing and used to love seeing local people pop in for a quarter of boiled ham and a pint.

We called Aunty Ann's father Granddad, and he was such a jovial and lovely man, so patient and kind to me. He would show us round his farm and let us have a ride on his donkey, which was shared with the neighbour down the road, when he was getting the peat in for the fires. I remember stroking the donkey and feeding him carrots and apples. When the bales of hay had to be brought in, it was great to run up them and then fall down again. Such innocent fun.

Today's kids are blasé when they get on and off planes, but to me returning annually to this little oasis was the highlight of my year. I loved it, and I would challenge anyone today to say sitting beside a swimming pool is better than running free through the fields and climbing trees.

Because Marie, my sister, was five years older than me, she left school just as I was starting. It left me a bit vulnerable, to be honest, because there was no big sister to stick up for me when I got bullied and, because of my glasses, that did happen quite regularly. I wanted to make lots of friends, but I was never one of the popular ones, so I stuck to one or two local girls and that was it. St Teresa's was a nice little school and, of course, it was Catholic, so that suited everyone. There was Mass during the week and on Saints' Days, and regular lessons in the catechism. I remember the teachers being a good bunch, on the whole, and I enjoyed my education there. I was particularly good at art, and my talent for drawing developed at St Teresa's. Once, I took a picture home and my mum thought it was so good that she asked me if I had traced it. I hadn't, and now I can see it was a compliment, but back then I was a bit affronted!

What I really liked about St Teresa's was that it was a proper community school. You knew everyone – teachers, dinner ladies, cleaning staff, caretakers – and because everyone was local you couldn't get away with bad behaviour. The teachers seemed a lot older as a group than they are now, and I feel they had the life skills necessary to teach at primary-school level. I look at teachers today and they seem so young, almost too young to have had much experience of the real world.

Like thousands of others, I didn't pass my 11-plus exam, so it was off to secondary modern for me, which in my case was St Patrick's RC High School in Eccles. As at primary school, our Marie had left before I started, but at least this time I knew a few people from St Teresa's who were also going up to 'big school'. I had to catch a bus there, which was a bit of a shock at the start because I'd been used to leaving the house at 8.45 a.m. to get to St Teresa's. Another surprise was just how many kids were there: when you're 11 and just starting secondary school, it seems as though you're surrounded by thousands of older, bigger children. I know I felt like that. Senior schools were very tough in those days; there was a lot of bullying and threats made that went unnoticed, and when it was noticed the strap was dished out, but at least when the final bell rang you could go home and forget about it. Today's kids have to face bullying online and by text message, so there is no escape. It's a 24/7 culture and kids bear the brunt of that.

My favourite subjects were art and history. I loved history and was soon top of the class. Sadly, it wasn't to last. I'd got on well with my history teacher and worked hard for him, but in the final two years our history class was taken by another teacher whose specialist subject was sport, particularly rugby. So he spent the next two years talking to the lads about rugby, and history went out of the window. I suppose I needed to pull my socks up at school, but it didn't quite work out that way. Mum and Dad wanted me to do well, and I'd be hung, drawn and quartered if I got a bad report or one of the teachers said something negative about me.

As I was getting ready to leave school at 16, our Marie had already started a career in nursing and so I had a lot to live up to. She was the clever one, but also the rebel, whereas I was quieter: the younger child who observes what the older one is doing and either follows her or goes along another path. It was easier to keep my head down and be obedient. I was shy and had a horror of making a spectacle of myself. That trait remained with me, and I can't believe how I've changed over the years to be able to do the things I do, because, believe me, they didn't come naturally.

My parents always encouraged me to work, because they believed that you got out what you put in, and when I was about 12 I got a Saturday job in the local greengrocer's shop. I'd already tried a paper round, but I was useless. I didn't like hauling a load of heavy papers around in the Manchester rain and they usually ended up in a soggy mess. So I gave that up and started at the greengrocer's, which was more fun, and the money I earned came in handy for buying clothes. I tell my three girls now that I used to pay half for an outfit one week and pick it up the following week when I had the rest of the money. They find it hard to believe that any girl these days would wait a week for a new dress!

When I left school, I immediately went out looking for a job. Secretly, I harboured ambitions of going to art college, but it wasn't to be. I just followed the route most young people did in those days and started looking for work. That said, there wasn't much going at the time. Britain was in the economic doldrums, and, although I looked hard, I couldn't find anything I wanted to do. I signed on the dole, bringing home the princely sum of £10 a week, until my mum found me a job in a local chippy. It's not great for a teenager's social life to come home smelling of chip fat, but it was a means to an end and I was glad to have found a job.

My plan was to follow my sister into nursing, so I applied and was selected to sit the entrance exam. My dad took me, and I was full of optimism until I arrived at the hall and discovered there were just two places for ninety-four candidates. There were a lot of grammar-school girls in for the exam, and I knew I wouldn't be one of the two lucky ones. I was right, but that didn't stop me feeling mortified afterwards. Our Marie tried to comfort me by telling me that my first experiences as a nurse would involve 'a lot of mopping up', as she put it, and, while she was being kind, she knew how bitterly disappointed I was. Deep down, I felt a failure and again second best to my brighter, cleverer and more popular big sister.

So it was back to the drawing board, and I began to look around for other jobs. I had an idea that I could try office work, and when I spotted a position for an admin assistant at an advertising company in Manchester, I went for it — and got the job. I couldn't have been more pleased. The offices were in Deansgate, smack in the middle of Manchester and right next to Granada Studios. My role was to place adverts in the *Manchester Evening News* and other publications, and I was quickly promoted to the accounts department. I should have been over the moon, but I was working in an all-female department and I found it a very bitchy place to be. The backbiting was unbelievable, especially when I got promoted, and the stress of it actually made me ill with bronchitis. Of course, it wasn't called stress in those days, but that's what it was. We had a female boss and you would've thought she'd have sensed the atmosphere, but she seemed blind to it.

So, once again, I looked through the paper's job adverts. I eventually found a job in the city's courts – not from an ad but through a friend of Mum's who worked there. The job was based in a typing pool, typing criminal-charge sheets. I hadn't done a lot of typing, even though I'd been to night school to learn it, so I had to get myself up to speed quickly. Again, it was an all-female office, but the women were much friendlier than the previous lot. The work was enjoyable too, and soon I started to become fascinated with the law and the legal process. It wasn't something I'd experienced before, but I liked the buzz around the courts and the constant stream of characters that flitted in and out.

After a few years, I went for a promotion and became a committal court assistant, helping the court clerks in all kinds of criminal hearings. I'd take down witness statements and type them up for use in later hearings. I loved being in court, watching the theatre going on all around me. I wanted to be a court clerk myself, but you had to be a solicitor and I didn't think I had the capability to become one. People from my background didn't put much faith in education after 16; getting a job was more important and that's what I did, of course. Even so, I wanted to prove to myself that I could understand the law academically, and some years later I passed O level in Law at night school.

When I was about 18, we moved to Warrington. Dad never really felt at home in Irlam, and he experienced heart problems as the years passed. The Victorian house, with its steep stairs and nooks and crannies, was becoming too much for him, so it was decided we'd move to a more modern house. Mum and Dad had friends in Warrington, so they decided to settle in what was known as the 'new town', a huge residential development close to the M6 and M62. The new house was much easier to maintain, and they decided to rent rather than buy. I was upset at leaving Irlam; I'd spent most of my childhood and nearly all of my teenage years around there and I was leaving many friends behind. But by this time I'd met a lad that I was serious about, and because he was from St Helens, we were actually moving closer to where he lived. Besides, it was an easier journey into Manchester for me, so I wasn't leaving a lot behind except memories.

Now, in the first flush of love, I'd become engaged to this boy, but like many teenage relationships ours was a bit fickle and it soon fizzled out. We were simply too young to be engaged and thinking about marriage and all of that. I was upset and off boys for a while, but luckily I had my big sister Marie's shoulder to cry on. I wasn't much of a pub or nightclub person, preferring to see one or two friends at a health club or for a coffee and then go home. But Marie was keen to take me out with her boyfriend Mark, whom she later married. 'It'll do you good,' she said.

On Saturday nights, Mark was a DJ at a club in Eccles, Manchester, so one night we got dolled up and Dad drove us over to the club. Always more outgoing than me, Marie and Mark had got to know a few people who came in most Saturdays. One of them was one of the club's other DJs and she said it would be a laugh.

It was certainly that. Marie introduced me to the DJs and I got chatting to the tall, fair-haired one during breaks between records. When I say 'chatting', I mean he was telling jokes, having a laugh and generally winding me up in the best way possible. His name was Garry Newlove, he had it all and I was immediately attracted to him.

TWO

Finding Newlove

In Salford, in the early '60s, just round the corner from where I grew up, Garry Newlove had played with his friends in the cobbled streets of Ordsall. He was two years older than me and wouldn't have paid much attention to a little girl wearing glasses and clutching her favourite black doll. I can't say I'd have noticed him either, although I do recall his best friend from the time, a lad called Michael. Garry's family were Salfordians through and through, and there were a lot of them. His mum was one of eleven. Garry was the youngest of three, and I mean youngest: his sister, Pat, was a full eighteen years older, while his brother, Keith, was twelve years Garry's senior.

Garry's father had been a fire warden during the Second World War and after one particularly bad raid on Manchester he failed to come home the following morning. Garry's mum searched hospitals all over the area for him, before eventually discovering him in the worst place a wife could find her husband: the local hospital mortuary. He'd been put there with other victims of the raid, but on closer inspection it was discovered that he was still breathing, despite terrible head injuries. A metal plate was put into his skull and he survived, but for the rest of his life he suffered from bad headaches and couldn't bear loud noises. Still, he worked hard all his life, as did Garry's mum, who cooked for the staff at Manchester's central post office. She died of stomach cancer in 2002 and, having a lifelong hatred of hospitals, fought it to the end. She was admitted to St Ann's Hospice in her final days, but not long after she arrived Garry received a phone call. 'Would you please come and pick your mother up,' the voice at the other end said, 'she cannot settle to stay here.' She was a fighter all right, and her family's anchor. When she passed away, the family was never the same again. Sadly, I also know how that feels.

Like me, Garry looked up to his older siblings, but the gap between them was huge. He made his own friends around Salford, as well as trying to follow his brother and sister around, playing gooseberry. A bright lad, he suffered from a bit of bullying at primary school, but he socked it to his critics when he passed his 11-plus and went to Salford Grammar School. He was happy-go-lucky, and he remained so all his life, but he was no slouch in the brain department. He passed 11 O levels and was accepted into art college. He was a talented artist who could create the most realistic portraits. Tragically, Garry's dad died just as he was setting out in life, so he had to leave college and come home to work and support his mum. That was how it was among working-class people, and Garry accepted it. He worked at the post office alongside his mum for a while, then went on to a pharmaceutical company before getting a job in the industrial-heating trade.

Much as he enjoyed his job, steel pipes and heating pumps weren't what you'd call his passion in life. That was reserved for music. He adored music, collecting records obsessively and, when he was old enough, going out to work as a DJ. He spent every Saturday sifting through Manchester's record shops, looking for hard-to-get 12-inch singles, which he'd pile against the walls of his bedroom. At weekends, he and his mate Pete would DJ in nightclubs around Manchester, playing all the latest disco, soul and funk music that was so popular in the '70s and early '80s. He was naturally sociable and outgoing, and always had a good line in dry humour, so DJ-ing was the perfect part-time occupation for him.

Garry was 6 ft 2 in. to my 5 ft 5 in. He was tall and blond with very shiny teeth and green eyes. He always had a sparkle in his eyes and had a witty sense of humour. He had immaculate hair and was very trendy, even down to his white shoes! Those were the days of shoulder pads and white jackets, rolled-up sleeves and long wavy hair, just like Wham! I thought when I first set eyes on Garry on that night out with our Marie that he was a bit of all right. But I did tell myself to watch him, because his sense of humour made him a magnet to women and he loved being the centre of attention.

Even so, you can imagine my disappointment when, on the way home, our Marie gave me some bad news.

'That Garry's got a girlfriend,' she said. 'He's spoken for. So be careful.'

'Don't worry,' I said. 'I'm not rushing into anything, especially not with blokes who've got girlfriends. Nice though, wasn't he?'

Marie agreed, but as far as we were both concerned he was spoken for, and that was that. So I was a bit shocked when I came in from work a few days later and my dad told me someone called Garry had rung up.

'What did he want?' I asked

'How should I know?' Dad replied. 'We didn't get into any chit-chat. He says to ring him.'

Dad passed me a scrap of paper with a Manchester number

on it. I don't know how Garry had got ours: maybe through his DJ mate.

A few days later, he rang again, and for the second time I didn't call him back. When he rang a third time and my dad answered, I felt I had no choice but to see what he wanted.

'For the love of God, ring him back, our Helen,' my dad said, 'and put him out of his misery. Mine too!'

I fished the crumpled piece of paper from my bag and rang the number. A female voice answered.

'Who is it?' she demanded when I asked if Garry was there.

'My name's Helen,' I said, feeling slightly intimidated by this fierce-sounding woman. 'Garry asked me to ring him.'

'Did he now? Well, he's asleep on the sofa. He's just got in from work and had his tea but I will try and wake him up.'

All of a sudden this slurred voice came down the line: 'Hello?'

'Hiya, it's Helen,' I said. 'You've been trying to get hold of me and I thought I'd better give you a call back.'

'Erm . . . have I?' he said.

'Yes, you have! So what is it you want?' I demanded.

He laughed. 'Oh, aye! Forgot about that. Anyway, I was just ringing to see if you fancied coming out for a drink some time?'

I did, and I wanted to tell him that. Instead, I reminded him about his girlfriend. But I thought to myself it might not be all it seemed and would see what he had to say.

Well, we did go out. I met him at a bar in Manchester and he was as witty, funny and good-looking as I'd remembered him being from the club. I don't think I'd ever laughed as much in my life and I was hook, line and sinkered by him. My cheeks were aching with all the laughing that I did. But, soon, I steered the conversation to the girlfriend. I needed to know the score. If he just wanted a bit of fun on the side and would then go running back to her, he could forget it.

'We're not seeing much of each other. It's fizzling out. Honestly, it is.'

'Well, if it's what you say it is, you'd better tell her. If you want to see more of me, that is.'

He said he did, and he said he'd sort it out. I waited, not holding my breath. I liked Garry a lot, but I didn't know him well enough yet to trust him.

After about four days, he got in touch to tell me that he'd spoken to her and, although she wasn't pleased, she accepted it was over.

'So that's it,' he said. 'Now, when are you up for going out?'

He'd done what I asked, so I could hardly say no even if I'd wanted to – which I didn't.

That Saturday, he came to pick me up in his car, one of those big 1970s Ford Granadas. I'd never been in anything like it, as we'd always had smaller car models such as Fiestas and that type of thing, but Garry loved his cars and was out to impress. And he definitely did that. I was laughing as we sped off down the street, and for the next 20-odd years Garry Newlove made me laugh almost every day. We hit it off so well. We both had a love of art in common, and music, although his knowledge was so much better than mine. Even now, I could tell you that I like such and such a song, but I've no idea who it's by. Garry would always know, and probably own the flipping record too!

Gradually, I got to know his family, and discovered that his dad had passed away just a year or so before we'd met. I wondered if his mum would accept me, but gradually she warmed towards me and we got on well. She would also be a fantastic mother-in-law and wonderful nana to all our children.

I was surprised, though, when I found out just how much she looked after Garry. She had his tea on the table the minute he walked in from work and she wouldn't ever disturb him during his power nap. If he was going out, she'd run a bath for him and put his clothes on the bed. Coming from a house with no young men in it, I found this amazing. Mind you, I vowed that, if we ever got married, *I* wouldn't be doing all that. It also turned out that my mum remembered Garry's brother from our times in Salford, so we had a lot of fun trying to find out who we knew in common.

My social life really took off when I met Garry. From having quiet times with my girl mates, suddenly I was being whisked around discos across Manchester and beyond. I was having fun and staying out late, something I'd never done much of before. I remember one evening when Garry rang and asked me to go out. It was a Monday or a Tuesday, certainly a work night, and I was attending night school that evening. I told him I was sorry, but night school only finished at 9 p.m. and then it was bedtime for me.

'Bed? I don't think so,' he said. 'Clubs only start at 11 p.m. You'll be fine. I'll come over to pick you up.'

I'll never forget the look on Dad's face when Garry came over, dressed in all the trendiest early 1980s gear, complete with cap-sleeved T-shirt and a pair of white shoes. He was very toned and looked fantastic to me. But those shoes! The following day, Dad gave me a bit of a talking to, because I'd only come in at 5 a.m. and I had to be at work just a few hours later. But by this time I was 20 years old and Garry and I were courting steadily, so Dad didn't go too overboard. Mum and Dad liked Garry a lot and they knew he was an honest bloke. Mind you, Dad never forgot those white shoes . . .

Garry always had a strong romantic streak. He was a very tactile person, and we always walked together holding hands.

He knew that I loved soft toys and would buy me my favourite Care Bears. We went on our first holiday to Salou. Not that we went on holiday *together*, of course. It's normal for boyfriends and girlfriends to do that now, but 30 years ago it was still frowned upon as 'not respectable'. I went with a mate, and, by sheer coincidence, so did Garry! It turned out we'd both booked the same week in the same area, but neither of us knew until he mentioned it. Anyway, it was a good job we weren't sharing the same hotel room, as the place he was staying was an absolute dump. Talk about *Fawlty Towers* . . . He had gone with his best friend Graham Timms and so, of course, booking a holiday with two lads meant shoving them in any old hole. Their bedroom had green fungus on the walls and the toilets were no better. Their mattresses felt like they were filled with sand. It was just unbelievable. But we all had a great holiday, and maybe the Spanish sun made Garry even more romantic as he'd even talked about our getting engaged after only four months together.

Sadly, after a while, Garry's addiction to DJ-ing began to cause a rift between us. He really got into it and we were travelling miles every weekend to different clubs. It was fun at first, but after a while I found myself just sitting on the sidelines while he played clubs in Prestwich, Rochdale, Bury and beyond. In short, I got bored with it. I didn't want to spend every Saturday night watching Garry play records, and we began to drift apart. So we split up for a few months. I was devastated. What I didn't know was that Garry had been phoning my mum during the break, wondering if I would give him a second chance. I was prepared to, but I said he'd have to pack in the DJ-ing or it was never going to work.

Not long after we got back together, he asked me to marry him and of course I said yes. It would be the start of a journey through life – and, sadly, death too.

THREE

Forsaking All Others

It was 1985, and as we'd already been together a few years, we didn't want a particularly long engagement, and decided to get married the following year. We went to a small jeweller in Manchester city centre to choose a ring. Eventually, we settled on a simple gold band solitaire diamond ring for me and a signet diamond for Garry. Together, they cost £300, which in those days was a lot of money, the top salary being £20,000.

The next question was: where would we live? I didn't particularly want to go back to Irlam or Salford, so Warrington was a strong option. Then again, did we want to live so close to my family or should we live closer to Garry's family? I was happy to look further afield, and I was excited when Garry's sister told us she was moving from Sale, an upmarket suburb just outside Manchester, and that her house would be on the market. Sadly, neither of us was earning a particularly good wage and the house was out of our price bracket, so it was back to the drawing board. Warrington was still expanding then, and new estates seemed to be springing up every week. So we went to have a look and eventually put down a deposit on a three-bed semi that wasn't yet built. It seemed good value, although central heating and a garage were extra, and it was only ten minutes from my parents' place in Padgate. The mortgage was agreed and we signed the paperwork. It gave us both a buzz to watch it being built brick by brick and we took photos every time a new doorframe had been completed! We spent many a happy Sunday that year nipping over to see it taking shape. The house was due to be ready for June 1986, the month set for our wedding, so that suited us just fine.

The other question was: where would we get married? Being a Roman Catholic, I was keen to marry in St Teresa's Church in Irlam, the church I'd attended most of my life. Our Marie had been married there too, and on the day of her wedding, as it was only a five-minute walk from our house, we asked the bridal-car driver if he'd take us round the block for a bit. To the surprise of the guests waiting for the bride's arrival, we drove right past the church and did a couple of turns round the local Kwik Save car park before heading back to St Teresa's! Now we'd moved from Irlam we wouldn't have that problem, and I was sentimentally attached to the place, so Irlam it would be.

That was all very well, but there was Garry to consider. He was raised Church of England, and, back then, the Catholic Church was very keen for non-Catholics to convert – or at least have a good understanding of the faith – before getting married in a Catholic church. Also, as I was living in Warrington, I was officially in the Diocese of Liverpool and St Teresa's was in the Diocese of Salford, so I had to ask for permission from Liverpool to get married 'over the border', so to speak. What a palaver just for one day!

After the worry about whether I would get permission through in time, because of a postal strike, it was eventually granted, so the next step was pre-marriage 'instructions' at St Teresa's. To be honest, it felt a bit of a joke. Garry and I thought it would be to do with the religious faith and the morals behind it and all of that, but, in fact, there was more about owning a house and married life in general than anything else. Father Birmingham, the priest who was going to marry us, was a good sport and tried to make the process as light as possible. We agreed to raise any children we might have as Catholics, which didn't quite happen (sorry, Father Birmingham . . .) and we attended pretty much all of the lessons. So we did our duty and looked forward to the wedding, which was fixed for 21 June.

I was 24 and Garry was 26, and by this time we'd moved into our house. Due to a mild winter, it had been built quicker than we thought, and by February 1986 it was ready to move into. It seemed silly to keep paying board to our parents while we had a mortgage, so we simply moved in together. I was nervous about my parents' reaction, particularly my dad's, but he understood our situation and was fine with it. I had already guessed Dad was OK when I saw the boxes on the landing full of all my cuddly toys and things that he could not wait to see the back of!

As well as the wedding, the other highlight of the summer of '86, at least for Garry, was the World Cup being held in Mexico. He was riveted, especially during the England games, and as the wedding drew nearer and the preparations became feverish, it was often hard to drag him away from the telly. He wasn't alone. One evening, we went over to St Teresa's to rehearse the ceremony. One of the big fixtures was on that night, so Garry and Father Birmingham immediately struck up a conversation about football until I intervened, wanting to get to the important stuff. We started the rehearsal – walking down the aisle and signing the register – and everything was going well until there was some sort of commotion from the back of the altar. Father Birmingham went to investigate and he came back out to say that whoever was playing (typically, I've forgotten!) had scored a goal. He and Garry rushed through the church to the priest's house to watch the replay, leaving me standing there like a lemon.

Football fever aside, the wedding went like a dream. It really was the happiest day of my life. My dad tickled me by talking to the wedding-car driver on the way to the church about its fuel intake. He loved cars and was impressed with this beauty. Where was the father/daughter heart-to-heart everyone said happened in those last precious moments alone? Even Father Birmingham overlooked me when, after greeting us both at the altar, he leaned over and complimented Garry on his choice of suit! 'Lovely cut, Garry, very smart.' I laughed and coughed for him to look over at me and he said very hurriedly, 'Of course, you look lovely too, Helen.'

My dress was white with lace short sleeves and lots of layers, but it wasn't too puffy. I was definitely not a meringue girl. My veil was ten feet long, so it was a challenge to keep my head up at all times. I had a tiara to hold it in place. At that time, it was fashionable to carry silk rather than fresh flowers. My bouquet included pink and white roses and freesias because I love the smell. Even though they weren't real, I imagined the fragrance as I walked down the aisle. My bridesmaids were Marie, who was my matron of honour, and my cousin and Garry's nieces. They wore baby-blue lace, gypsy-style off-the-shoulder dresses and they carried the same coloured bouquets. All the guests were dressed in their best. There were hats all around and some people even wore gloves, although it was the hottest and longest day of the year.

It wasn't an over-the-top wedding by any means, but our parents were kind enough to pay for the evening reception, as well as the flowers and photographer. We had around 200 guests and a great night do. I really didn't want Garry to DJ at our own wedding. It was our day and I didn't want memories of me just standing there while he entertained everyone else. Garry arranged to have a friend of his work the decks, but as it turned out he cried off with a bad back a day or two before, so a replacement was sent – and he really wasn't very good on the night. The evening just wasn't getting going and I knew Garry was itching to get on there and do the business.

I asked him again not to do it. Garry dug his heels in and three hours into our wedding we were having our first row as a married couple. Finally, we compromised. Even I could see that he had a point and reluctantly I gave in. He could go on for a bit and warm it up, but then he had to let the other guy take over. So that's what happened and soon everyone was on the dance floor at last. When Garry came off, he was delighted the party was going so well and, like all the best parties, it carried on very late into the night. We were invited to our neighbours' house for post-wedding drinks and a whole entourage came along, including Garry's boss, Wally. Garry had been good all day and had hardly touched a drop, but now it was time for him to let his hair down. He and Wally attacked the beers and Southern Comfort, and it took Garry two full days to get over it.

We spent our honeymoon in the glamorous setting of a caravan in Rhyl. It belonged to my uncle and he'd lent it to us as a wedding present. We were trying to save money, as we had a new house and a new car, so a honeymoon abroad wasn't an option, but at least this was a break. Besides, we were just married and very much in love, so who cared where we were? We were having fun and the weather was good too, so it didn't matter. We went to Llandudno one day and sat among the pensioners as they ate their ice creams and listened to a choir on the seafront.

'Eh, this'll be us one day,' Garry said, nodding to the elderly couples. 'How about that, love?'

'Well, that's great,' I said, 'but don't think I'm coming back here for my silver wedding anniversary. You can take me abroad for that one!'

He laughed, and promised that he would. June 2011 – which would be our 25th anniversary – seemed a world away. Sadly, Garry would be unable to fulfil that promise made on a hot summer's afternoon so long ago.

FOUR

In Sickness and in Health

After our honeymoon, it was back to reality, which, for me, held something unpleasant and unexpected. I'd been having some gynaecological problems and, just six weeks after the wedding, I ended up having to go to hospital. I was diagnosed with a cyst on my ovary and the doctors thought it very unlikely that I'd ever have children. 'Maybe Mother Nature will work it out,' they said, 'but try not to be too disappointed if it doesn't happen.'

Disappointed? I was devastated, like any newly married woman would be. You never think twice about having children. But maybe I should've known better. My mum had also had problems having Marie and me, so maybe I'd inherited something genetic from her. Garry loved kids too and always spoiled his nieces and nephews, so the news was hard to hear.

However, a year or so later, I discovered I was pregnant. Since the cyst and the doctor giving his opinion, our hopes had been raised then cruelly dashed twice, and I was resigned to the thought that maybe I'd never hold our child in my arms. So I didn't want to get too excited, and, although I felt sick, I was determined to go on the holiday that Garry had booked for us. When I came back, I went to the clinic and they confirmed the pregnancy to our great joy. Third time lucky! In May 1989, I gave birth by Caesarean to Zoe, our first child, in Trafford General Hospital, where our Marie worked as a nurse. I had spent the previous 12 weeks flat on my back with all sorts of complications. It was a hell of a long time, especially for Garry, who just wanted to begin family life. Mind you, he kept the house lovely and clean until I arrived home with Zoe and the full weight of newborn-baby chaos hit us like a bolt from the blue!

I couldn't believe she was mine, as she was so perfect. Zoe was a long baby, very fair and blue-eyed. The midwife told me all babies' eyes are that colour, but Zoe's never changed. She was a nosy baby, wanting to know what everyone was doing. She was my parents' first granddaughter (Marie had already had her son Adam). Garry's mum, Ellen, doted on her so much that she wanted to have her one day a week to look after, even though she was only a few months old. I was apprehensive at first, as I thought Zoe would be too much. Ellen was 70 years of age, after all. But she proved me wrong and was a model childminder, and I had no hesitation leaving my baby in her capable hands. Their time together was very precious and the loving bond remained as strong until she died. When the others came along, Ellen loved them just as much and I was lucky to have such a wonderful mother-in-law, and grandmother for my children.

We were very much looking forward to starting proper family life. Garry was offered a new job the same day I had Zoe and he was working hard to make a good impression. Although he used to come home from work very tired, he always found time for Zoe, and later her little sisters, bathing them and putting them to bed. Because my health wasn't too good, he did over and above what many working dads would have done, but he was a very natural father and never complained once, even when he was dog-tired. He would get up to feed them at night and play with them all weekend, giving me a break. He was so good like that. Naturally, they adored him in return.

We tried to get on with life, but very quickly I became ill again, this time with gall bladder problems, and I was sent back to hospital. While there, a consultant gave me a full examination and said that I wasn't in a good way, gynaecologically speaking. 'You were lucky to have Zoe,' he said. 'If you're planning to have any more, I wouldn't put it off for too long.'

Well, I wasn't planning a huge family, but Garry and I both wanted more than one. So along came Danielle on 4 February 1992, and it felt incredible to have had another baby. Hers was an easy birth compared to Zoe's, which was wonderful for me after all the hospital drama I'd gone through previously: I had another Caesarean, but this time it wasn't as traumatic and I left for home a few days later. Ecstatic, we took her home to meet her big sister and we just couldn't believe how lucky we were to have two healthy beautiful daughters.

Danielle's temperament was different from Zoe's; she was always asleep. She was very much a textbook baby, sleeping, eating well and sleeping again. Even now she can sleep for England. Danielle was dark haired, with big blue eyes and a smile that would melt you. Zoe treated her like a doll and loved to bathe her with Garry in the evening. Daddy always came home at night for the bedtime routine, knowing two young daughters were gurgling for his attention.

In September 1992, we went on holiday to Cyprus. Garry hadn't been feeling particularly well, but it was thought he had a stomach ulcer and he didn't have any tests. He was still feeling rough on holiday, but he found that if he ate he suddenly felt much better. It was a bit bizarre, but we managed to have a good holiday anyway.

When we came back, one afternoon Garry announced that he was going off to help paint a friend's house. When he returned later that day, he looked terrible.

'What've you been up to?' I said. 'Have the paint fumes got to you or something?'

He wiped sweat off his brow. He'd gone a horrible grey colour. Even when his stomach cramps were at their worst, he'd never looked as bad as this.

'I dunno,' he replied. 'I had a funny turn in the car on the way over there. I ate a banana and I don't think it's agreed with me.'

I said he needed to see a doctor, but he disagreed. He was never one for bothering doctors or taking tablets – typical bloke, really. My mum came round and, canny woman that she is, thought he'd gone a funny yellow colour. She told me to phone the doctor immediately, which I did. He called round and took a look at Garry but couldn't say for sure what it was. If his condition didn't improve in a few days, the doctor said, he should be admitted to hospital.

Well, we did not have to wait a few days as Garry had a terrible night and he just wasn't himself – constantly hot and sticky, and a terrible colour. I told him he had no option but to go in. If his stomach ulcers were playing him up this badly, he needed to have them sorted out, and quickly. So off we went, and they arranged for Garry to have an endoscopy to determine what the problem was. Garry asked the doctor to make sure that he gave him enough anaesthetic to knock him out as he really didn't want to be awake while they were doing it. They told him not to worry and assured him it would be all sorted, but, unfortunately, he wasn't given a big enough dose of anaesthetic and he was still awake as they took him to have the procedure. In a panic, he lashed out at one of the doctors and caused a terrible commotion. Finally, he was given the correct dose and the endoscopy went ahead.

Within a week, we were called back to the hospital for the results. We sat and sat for what felt like hours while other patients went in and out to see the consultant. Finally, we were called in. The consultant greeted us warmly, inviting us to sit down. Then his manner changed, and he became serious and solemn.

'What I have to tell you will come as a shock,' he said, 'but you do need to know now so that we can move quickly. I'm sorry to say, Garry, that you have stomach cancer.'

The consultant held up the X-ray of Garry's stomach against a light-box and pointed out a series of cauliflower-shaped blooms.

'Don't be daft,' I said, on the verge of panic. 'That's not cancer. It can't be. Surely it's just a build-up of acid or something?' I looked at Garry. He was just staring straight ahead in complete silence. 'Oh my God,' I said. 'You mean it, don't you? He's got cancer. But he can't have . . . he's only 32. It can't happen so young, can it?'

'I'm afraid it can,' the consultant replied. His voice was calm and steady. He must've broken this type of news so many times, and witnessed the shock and horror of those on the receiving end. 'But, as I said, we need to move quickly. The only option is a partial stomach removal.'

'What, *now*?' I said.

'No, no – not yet. You can go home today and try to absorb this news. We'll get a team of people together and we'll have you back within three weeks. There is one other thing – you will have to sign a consent form giving us the right to remove the whole stomach if we think that's necessary. Hopefully, it won't be.'

'OK, thanks,' Garry said, as though he'd been told his car needed a new exhaust or something. I couldn't believe how calmly he'd taken the news. He was shocked, of course, but there was a core of steel running through him, which became evident in the agonising three-week wait before the operation.

Garry was the bravest man alive during that time. He had

two infants and a wife and was only just in his 30s. Before the diagnosis, he'd had all his life ahead of him and now he was facing a very uncertain future. Despite all that, he remained positive and as cheerful as possible, even when he reminded me that he once said he thought he'd die before the age of 50.

'You daft bugger,' I said. 'You're not going to die. You'll get better. You have to; you can't leave me with two kids.'

''Course I'll get better,' he replied. 'I'll be fine. Don't worry.'

Somehow – and I don't really know how – we got through those three weeks. I made Garry eat lots of carrots, even though he hated them, because I'd heard they were full of anti-cancer properties. Poor fella, I'm surprised he didn't turn a deep shade of orange during that period, but I'd have done anything to make him better. I was only just thirty and was staring at the prospect of being widowed with two little girls to look after. This nightmare could not be happening to us. I spent many hours talking to God and making deals to get Garry through the worst. We would help him get back on his feet and have a healthy life, no matter what it took. His mum was crushed and said, over and over again, that she wished it was her and not him. She kept saying that she did not want to have to bury her son before her. It was not right. Parents go before their children – that is the right order of life. That is why we have children, to live on after we have gone.

The day of the operation arrived. Garry was nervous (who wouldn't be?), particularly because he didn't like hospitals anyway. He was in theatre for five hours, and when he was opened up they found that the cancer had spread, so his whole stomach was removed, along with his spleen. The lower and upper bowel were attached, forming a pocket that made a 'new' stomach. After the operation, he was in intensive care for three days, wired up to all sorts of machines. I could hardly take in what was happening and cried constantly. One evening, during visiting time, he heard someone crying and he made me put my face close to his – he was as blind as a bat without his glasses – to see if it was me. But it wasn't; the noises were coming from a bedside nearby where someone had received bad news. I really didn't want to cry in front of him. My health visitor at the time said I was storing up the grief 'too deeply'. Perhaps I was, but for me it was a case of focusing on Garry to make sure he got better for all of us.

Mum and Dad, who loved him like a son, took over at night to look after the kids while Garry's mum and I went to sit with him in the hospital. There was a stream of people coming and going: all his family and my family taking it in turns to try to keep his spirits up.

After intensive care, he was taken to a regular ward, where the 'care' he received nearly killed him. He was in agony and wasn't given any pain relief, because they couldn't find the machine that would allow him to self-administer it. Vital injections were missed too, and when our GP found out he wiped the floor with the hospital, telling them that if Garry contracted a cold he could be dead within 12 hours. The upshot of all this was that Garry begged to come home and, although he should've been in for six weeks, he got out after ten days. Before the operation, he was a fit 13.5-stone 32-year-old bloke; now he was down to 8 stone and looked like an old man.

I was pleased to have Garry back home, although he was having to learn how to eat again and how to live as a survivor of a life-threatening illness and a huge operation. He was so thin that he could feel the tablets in the place his stomach used to be, and that feeling made him physically sick so he couldn't keep them down. He was living on two cream crackers a day because any more than that would go straight into his bloodstream and knock him right out. Eating anything was agony for him, and to his dying day he slept on his hands and knees after his evening meal to make sure the food had gone into his system. All that and the demands of two very small children was enough to get anyone down, but we tried to remain as cheerful as possible and look on the bright side. At least he was alive, and every day of life after that operation was a bonus.

The children could not understand why Daddy was unable to cuddle and carry them. They just saw him lying on the sofa resting and did not know any better. Even though he would wince with pain, he would still put his arms around them and snuggle into them. He loved them dearly and tried to show them in a different way he was still the same old Dad.

Slowly, Garry started to get better. He put on weight – although he never became fat – and at Christmas we held a party for him, which he enjoyed, even if he looked utterly knackered. That year, I bought him a keyboard and a basketball net and stand. He loved basketball and he'd played a lot when he was younger. I will always remember that year. It seemed a miracle he was still with us, and I felt we really had fought and won a battle with death. After Christmas, we went for a break to the Lake District, while my mum and dad looked after the girls. He was tired and having trouble eating. He was also angry too, a kind of 'why me?' anger experienced by many people who have been through cancer. It wasn't an explosive, shouty anger that had everyone running for cover. His was directed inward: anger at his body letting him down, the unfairness of his illness, the thought it might take him away from the girls and me when we so desperately needed him. He fretted over every ache and pain and had to be constantly reassured, usually by me, that he would be fine.

After six months, Garry went back to work. Many people saw this as a brave decision, but the truth was we were hard up and it was a necessity. Benefits worked out at around £30 a week and we simply couldn't manage. His firm had also taken back his company car and replaced it with an old banger, so Garry's pride had taken a dent too. He loved his cars and he didn't want to drive some old wreck around. What had happened to him health-wise was bad enough. Our GP advised him not to rush back into full-time work, so Garry took his advice and went part-time at first.

Garry's illness totally changed our lives. A few months after he went back to work, we decided to move house. An insurance payout meant we now had no mortgage and so we were able to buy a thatched cottage in Great Sankey, the kind of house I'd always dreamed of living in. It looked like a picture on a box of posh biscuits. The warmth that you got from the Aga oven when you walked through the kitchen was just delightful. The cottage had oak beams, an inglenook fireplace and windows with small panes, which I never tired of washing and dressing with new curtains. I kept it like a pin and was so proud to be the owner of such a wonderful home. The girls had a room each with one to spare. We'd been through the worst, we thought, and now it was time to live out our dreams. Little did we know what was around the corner.

Garry was still getting aches and pains, and when these became more frequent he wasted no time in going back to the doctor. I thought they were just muscular, but our doctor was very good and wouldn't take any chances. Since Garry's diagnosis, he'd been advising all his patients under 40 to get strange pains properly checked out. So Garry was sent to the hospital for a scan and, once again, we were called into a consultant's office to find out the results.

I went with a lump in my throat but still expected the outcome to be a positive one. 'Lightning doesn't strike in the same place twice,' I told myself. 'It's impossible that something else can happen to Garry.'

The specialist we saw was horrible – cold, seemingly uncaring and totally detached from the patient's needs. He could've been talking to someone bringing their cat in. With barely a 'good morning', he pulled out the X-ray and pointed somewhere in the middle of Garry's body.

'Do you see these speckles here?' he said, showing us some white dots. 'Bad news, I'm afraid. You've got liver cancer.'

I couldn't have felt more shocked if the doctor had simply stood up and kicked me in the face. It was just 12 months since the last lot and this was potentially far worse. I didn't know a lot about liver cancer, but I knew that few people made much of a recovery from it, if they recovered at all.

'How long has he got?' I said, shell-shocked.

'Don't know,' said the consultant, without looking up. 'Three weeks? Three months? Three years? Who can say?'

With that, I burst into tears. I couldn't believe what I was hearing, nor the offhand way we'd been told the news. How would I cope with this? I didn't want to face again the prospect of being a widow with two young children. My mind was racing through all sorts of terrible possibilities. Garry was devastated. He'd fought so hard, and had endured so much pain, to get over the last lot. Now he had to face this. How horrible for him, and for us all.

The upshot was that we went back to our GP and were quickly referred to the Clatterbridge Centre for Oncology (now Clatterbridge Cancer Centre), which had just opened a clinic not far from Warrington. Garry was the first patient to see Mr Clark, the consultant. In contrast to the last doctor, Mr Clark was friendly and caring, and understood how we must be feeling. Before chemotherapy could start, Garry had to have more tests, and these were carried out at Clatterbridge. Again, I asked how long Garry would have to live and I was told it depended on the success (or otherwise) of the chemo. Obviously, it was going to be touch and go whether he would survive at all, but, again, we had to keep going until we knew exactly what we were facing.

The waiting time for the test results was about three weeks. This time round, Garry wasn't so positive about the prognosis. He was convinced he had terminal cancer, and no amount of my trying to persuade him otherwise would change his mind. The truth was that I thought he might have it too. So we went through three weeks of hell with a possible death sentence hanging over our heads while we tried to live as normally as possible, looking after our little ones.

Garry's brother, Keith, came with us to pick up the results. I knew I couldn't cope alone and so he offered us his support. As the three of us trooped into the consultant's room, my head was pounding and I thought I was going to be sick. The consultant looked agitated and uneasy. It could mean only one thing.

'I have something to say to you,' he said, 'and it isn't easy to say. For you, Garry, it's good news. You don't have liver cancer. Not a trace of it.'

'What?' he said. '*Not* got it? But the scans showed—'

'The scans showed nothing,' the consultant interrupted. 'I'm afraid a more junior member of staff interpreted the X-ray and they got it totally wrong. I can only say that I'm very, very sorry.'

Well, he wasn't as sorry as we were. I was livid. We'd just moved house and been busy making videos of us all so when the girls grew up they would be able to see what their daddy had looked like. Garry could've become so down and despondent about his future that he killed himself, and maybe us too if he'd chosen to do something stupid while driving. I never thought he would do that, but you don't know how despair will affect you. And it would all have been for nothing: for a set of results that were flawed. It sickened us, and we thought about suing, but we were told by a solicitor that it would cost thousands of pounds. This was before the days of 'no win, no fee', so it was totally out of the question. The solicitor said her advice wasn't 'classist', but that's exactly what it was. Only wealthy people could possibly afford to do it.

Garry had his liver scanned again, just to be on the safe side, and nothing at all was spotted. Anyway, shocked – and of course relieved – as we were, our lives were about to take another twist, which wouldn't leave a lot of time for pursuing legal cases. I was pregnant again. Hard to believe, given all the ups and downs, Garry's operation and my gynaecological problems, but there it was. We were to have our third child in a matter of months: our surprise baby.

On 11 November 1994, our third daughter, Amy, was born, by yet another Caesarean. This time it wasn't going to be as easy as it had been with Danielle. I'd had a hard pregnancy, feeling very nauseous and generally unwell, and Amy came at just 37 weeks. My spine was shot to pieces, and by the time of her birth I could hardly walk. I was so anaemic that if I'd carried her any further I'd have haemorrhaged and probably died. I was told to wait at least five years before thinking about having another one, but it didn't take much discussion between Garry and me to decide that enough was enough. We had three lovely daughters and we were happy with that. It would've been selfish to think otherwise. And tempting fate.

Amy always teases her siblings by saying she was the 'miracle' baby. My health was so poor I shouldn't have been able to conceive again let alone carry to full term. And Garry, by all laws, after the aggressive treatment for his cancer, should not have been able to father a child. In addition, back then, it was frowned upon to have three Caesareans – two was your lot. But here she was, simply perfect. Amy looked more like Zoe: they both had long limbs and the same colouring and features. Amy was very placid and enjoyed her food, which she still does. Her hair was curly, which I loved and she hated as she grew up.

Our three daughters enjoyed each other's company and I loved dressing them in the same style of clothes, all bright colours. Very girly and, oh, how I enjoyed those days when I had a say!

So, once again, we started to make a go of family life and, at last, things seemed to be settling down. Garry changed jobs a few times due to redundancies, so there were periods of stress, but nothing like it had been. We were the most normal family you'd ever imagine. The girls started to develop their personalities and we had great fun watching them grow up from toddlers to young schoolchildren. Zoe was studious and artistic. She loved drawing and colouring in, and jigsaws kept her occupied for hours. She was a nosy little kid, always wanting to know what was going on, and she didn't sleep much at night for fear she was missing something. Danielle was an easier baby, in that we could be up and dressed before she'd even woken up – well, at least until she was two, then she suddenly became much more lively. Amy gave us very few problems. Given what we'd been through, we were just glad she was around at all, and we were so grateful for her.

Garry was a great father, as I've mentioned (and no doubt will mention again as this story unfolds). He picked the girls up from school, St Philip's in Great Sankey, whenever he could and would very often make them their tea before bathing them and putting them to bed. He was very much a home bird, not one of those men who would stay out or pretend they were working to get away from the domestic duties. The simple fact was that he loved being around his family and we did everything together, even to the extent of going to the hairdresser's and dentist. At weekends, he loved nothing more than pottering about, playing with the kids and washing his car. Garry's mum came to stay with us occasionally, and most years we'd take off on a family holiday. When the kids started school, I went back to work part-time as a legal PA. Like so many families around the UK, we did what we did to get by. We were normal, average people who worked hard for what we had and enjoyed our family life. The life-threatening illnesses made us realise life was so short and precious, and we treasured every moment, making the most of our time together. Garry loved family life and lived for his three girls.

This could've gone on for years. Garry and I would've watched our girls grow up and move on with their lives. We would've had – and we did have – our ups and downs, just like any other couple, but we'd have got through them and hopefully enjoyed anniversaries, 18th and 21st birthdays, weddings, grandchildren and our own retirement and old age. Then again, who knows what life will bring? It might not have been that way at all. What I do know is that it can never be that way now, at least not as far as Garry is concerned. Life goes on, of course, but our family's life cannot be the same as it was. In a sense, it's at this point that the story of the Newlove family as it is today truly starts – the point where we left the cottage we'd lived in for thirteen years and moved to the Padgate area of Warrington. It would be the worst move of our lives.

FIVE

Trouble Brewing in Paradise

We decided to move for several reasons. The first was that we wanted to downsize a little and keep some money in the bank. Another reason was to be nearer to my mum and dad. By 2004, the year we moved to Padgate, they were older and needed more care. Being closer to them meant I could pop round regularly to make sure they were OK. Also, we were looking for an area that was more neighbourly than the development we'd been living on. It was fine, but there wasn't much mixing going on, and both Garry and I liked to know our neighbours. Perhaps it's because we were brought up in a more sociable environment and we wanted the same for ourselves as adults, and for the girls. Garry had reservations about moving into the Padgate area, but the four-bedroom detached house that had just been built was a reasonable price. Besides, I'd spent my late teens and early 20s around that area so it was familiar ground. When we moved in, we realised we had friendly neighbours who would think nothing of talking to you over the garden fence or inviting you round for a barbecue. That was what we wanted: a friendly 'hello' when you went off to work in the morning and a good natter at the weekend. It makes all the difference to a place, and I feel sad when communities fall apart for the lack of good neighbourliness.

It costs nothing and it means so much to those who value it. People might say it's old-fashioned to talk over the garden fence, but if it means a cohesive community that cares about its people, bring it on.

Anyway, we moved to Station Road North, Fearnhead, and quickly settled into the community there. It was about a ten-minute drive from our last house, and because Zoe and Danielle had well-established friendships at the high school there we decided it wasn't fair to move them, so Garry took them each morning and back home at night. Amy was coming to the end of her time at St Philip's primary school, so there was no point moving her either. I was still working in a solicitors' office in Manchester, so I'd be up and off for the train before the girls went to school. I'd get back to Padgate station at 6 p.m. and Garry would meet me with Amy and our dog, and we'd all walk home together.

There was a subway at the end of our road that was both a blessing and curse. It was blocked off to vehicles so it was very quiet as far as passing traffic was concerned, but it was also a magnet for youngsters who congregated underneath it. At first, this was nothing more than an occasional nuisance. They didn't seem to be kids local to the street and, more often than not, they would walk through it to get to the estate on the other side. I tried to be tolerant, even when there was a bit of noise going on. After all, I had two teenagers of my own and a pre-teen, so I knew what they could be like. When we first moved there, I didn't mind going through it to get to the shops, but after a while the girls starting complaining about the gangs of lads hanging around there, drinking from cans, writing on the concrete walls and generally being a bit foul-mouthed and abusive. I was disappointed more than anything else. I'd wanted us to live in a nice place and, having known the Padgate area for a long while, I thought we'd found somewhere that was more or less right for us. Still, it seemed a minor nuisance, nothing more. Of course, as time went on, I would change my mind about that completely.

For a year or so, give or take the odd bit of shouting and general noise underneath the subway, life was good in Station Road North. The girls were growing up beautifully and we were so proud of the way they were turning out. Garry and I would attend parents' evenings at school and were always pleased as Punch at the remarks about all three. They were industrious, sociable and engaged but, most importantly, polite and respectful.

Living there was handy for my mum's house, and my work in Manchester was just a short train ride away. Our weekends were structured. Garry continued the upkeep of the home, looking after the immaculate garden and washing our cars. Amy was his little apprentice, always there with a bucket and sponge, which she really loved to do. I looked after the girls and my parents; it was just like any other normal household.

Sadly, our little domestic bubble of happiness couldn't last. The problems connected with local youths began to escalate. Perhaps word had got round that the subway was a convenient shortcut. As the numbers increased, so did the severity of the anti-social behaviour. At first, it was litter in our and our neighbours' gardens. We were all fed up with picking up lager cans and food wrappers off our lawns and out of our flowerbeds. The increased noise was irritating too, but it was nothing on what was to come.

The new houses, including ours, had driveways only suitable for one car and we had two. Quite soon, cars parked on the street were suffering damage inflicted late at night. As a neighbourhood, we lost count of the times we woke up to find lager or urine down car bonnets or scratches along doors. It was very upsetting, particularly for Garry, whose passion for his cars never diminished. Sometimes he'd jump out of bed and look out of the window to see if anyone was approaching, but the attacks and the damage were random, and you never knew when it would flare up or die down. My nerves were shredded, and I'm sure anyone who has suffered or is suffering this sort of intimidation will recognise the high anxiety and stress this causes.

I now sit at conferences and listen to academics or unenlightened police officers brushing off 'minor anti-social behaviour' and agreeing between themselves that it is a nuisance but not actually a crime. I beg to differ! It erodes your peace of mind and can make you chronically emotionally and physically ill. It is relentless bullying and millions suffer. I remember speaking to one young girl in one of the neighbourhoods I am involved with in the inner city who asked me a question I could not answer. 'Why do we spend so much money, time and resources on worrying about international terrorism and attacks on our country when I'm suffering urban terrorism?' she said. If anybody can come up with an answer for her then let me know.

One evening, we'd been out to see some friends and were returning home, happy and relaxed after a good day out, when we were brought down to earth with a bump. We came back to discover a dozen lads and girls sitting on a telephone exchange box just by our drive. Later on, our next-door neighbour popped in and Garry asked him if everything was OK, as we were concerned about the group of youths at the telephone box. The neighbour said that he was fed up with the noise and that, although he had gone out to ask them to keep it down because of the baby being asleep, they wouldn't be quiet. So, in the end, he said he'd called the police. And, predictably enough, our neighbour was told there was little they could do and his call was 15th down the line. He said to Garry that he'd told them, 'If I went out with a baseball bat, you'd soon be down here.'

It was just one incident of many, but eventually our neighbour had had enough and moved his family away. With hindsight, how I wish to God we had seen the danger he saw and followed him.

I have to calm myself down by remembering that the police

most likely had a tick-box set of instructions from the Home
Office on how they should be spending their time. It was all about
meeting targets, and anti-social behaviour was not considered
criminal or even something to be taken that seriously. I am glad
that Garry's and other victims' cases have made them re-evaluate
this approach, and I hope I have contributed in some way to
addressing this terrible wrong.

We'd always had faith in the police. Now they seemed to have
shrugged their shoulders and washed their hands of the problem.
I started to worry about the girls walking through the subway and
even I became fearful of going through it in the evening. Others
felt the same way, which made it worse, because now this was a
no-go area that ordinary people were not allowed to enter. This
is what happens when you do not lay down the rules, from the
start, that no area in this country of ours should be out of bounds
because of safety issues and bullying behaviour. I hated the feeling
of having to cross the road to avoid groups of youths congregating
there, even though I knew in my heart that not all kids are bad.
All we could hope for was that they'd get bored and move on to
somewhere else, or simply just grow up and grow out of it.

Sadly, that wasn't to be. If anything, the nuisance became
worse. Damage to cars became a real problem among the
neighbours, but when people reported it to the police, all they
got was a crime reference number for insurance purposes. One
night I had my wing mirror smashed and the following day Garry
vowed that we'd move house. It might seem an extreme reaction
to something so petty but to me it was the culmination of so
much hassle and heartache. Of course, you discuss the major
decisions in your life as a family before taking the big steps, but
I was angry enough to go straight down to the estate agent's and
put the house on the market there and then. If only I'd done
that . . .

Eventually, and with little chance of the police doing anything, the residents banded together to find a solution. One day a leaflet popped through our doors from an active group of local residents who had tackled similar problems in their areas. A number of community meetings were held, at which local people could air their grievances, if nothing else. Garry was always sceptical and refused to attend, saying that nothing would change.

He was right in that respect, but it didn't stop me from going along with a handful of neighbours to see if there was anything we could do to make a difference. We knew there had been a similar community forum in nearby Cinnamon Brow because they'd suffered from the very same behaviour we were now enduring – late-night noise, swearing, mouthiness, damage to cars, etc. – but somehow they'd got rid of it. Of course, it became painfully clear just how they'd got rid of it when some of their representatives came to talk to us: the problems had simply been pushed on to us.

This particular meeting was packed, and there was a lot of argument from social-worker types about kids not having enough to do, and that residents were singling them out unfairly. What we were trying to say soon got lost in the row about what kids needed and how best to achieve it. But what about us? Weren't *we* the victims in all this? Why was no one listening to us? It is hard to write these words because I still have to deal with similar voices saying the same. For example, the apologists from the summer riots of 2011 seek to make excuses, blaming poverty, life chances and unemployment for bad behaviour. When will these people ever take responsibility? We all have a choice in life and it is the silent majority who must speak up now and reclaim the world we should all be living in.

By now it was early 2007, a very different time from the one Garry and I had grown up in. When we were children, there were only streets and scrappy bits of waste ground to play on, but we didn't use that as an excuse to annoy our neighbours. We made our own entertainment and we did not demand our rights, like so many young people do today. Compared to us, the kids who hung around Station Road North had loads of green space to play football or whatever. There was a local youth club, too. It was better than nothing and not having quite enough to do wasn't an excuse for doing what they did, and it still isn't.

We often discussed this. Garry and I and other responsible parents knew where our children were and what they were up to. Where were these young teenagers' parents? We'd be mortified if our girls were hanging around in bad company causing trouble. Did any one of these parents raise questions when their under-age kids came home at all hours drunk and drugged? And where were they getting hold of this booze?

I had grown up in this area since the age of 18, so it saddened me to see our local Co-op having to employ a security guard to keep out troublemakers. Every day, our local postmaster from the nearby post office diligently went out to clear all the litter that had been dropped there the night before. And still the meetings went on, everyone airing their views and telling each other how bad it was. Well, we all knew that but when was something going to be done about it? The police attended every meeting but these young lads were very much the junior ranks, or PCSOs, with very limited powers who always promised to 'feed back to the inspector' so that he could take a view. Fine words, but with the greatest respect we didn't want these boys passing on our complaints. We wanted the inspector – the man himself – down at the meeting. He never came.

At one meeting, some local elderly residents complained that a fence next to their garden which was running alongside a ginnel (alleyway) had been set on fire on several occasions. They were sick and tired of it and they wanted the person in charge of the fire service to attend the next meeting. So he did just that, along with the young police officers. He was still on his feet speaking to the residents when suddenly the screaming sound of a fire engine came closer and, of course, he went out to see what the problem was. Sadly, the fence was ablaze, which is what they'd dreaded.

How much more did we have to do to prove the level of suffering and fear we were being subjected to? As we were all gathered there, the kids started banging on the windows. To me, this was a direct insolent challenge to us as a community; even though they saw the police cars and the fire engines, they were so arrogant they taunted us with their behaviour. Showing no fear of authority was simply rubbing our noses in the problem. So this meeting disintegrated as the police went to remonstrate with the kids banging and the fire brigade went to deal with the fire. We were left looking at one another in disbelief. Now *surely* we would be finally listened to.

My campaigning today is always to beg agencies to look at prevention instead of responding to the after effects. By then it is too late. And I always, always fight to make them understand that they have to listen and build relationships with local people and bring them into the solutions of the problems that affect their lives.

The kids were laughing at us because they knew they were getting away with it. Numbers began to dwindle at the neighbourhood meetings due to the lack of action. Everybody wanted to see an inspector, or a few more officers on the streets, but we couldn't even take our complaints to the local police station because there wasn't enough staff there to respond to us in person. We had to write everything down and put it in a box in the local library for the beat bobby to collect. We asked the council to get rid of the graffiti in the subway and repaint it, and put litter bins in. Nothing happened.

We asked representatives of the local school to come to a meeting. I told them that their kids were hanging about at lunchtime, smoking under the subway and meeting older students or friends who were no longer in education. I felt they were at risk of being dragged into even worse behaviour as at times there were bottles of alcohol left in the subway. I was absolutely shocked when I was told that it was 'not our responsibility if they're off school premises'. I know it is an overused phrase but I do firmly believe in the old African idea that it takes a village to bring up a child. We cannot wash our hands and look the other way when young people are straying off the path that will lead them into being responsible good citizens. Of course, it is the responsibility of parents, grandparents, family and friends but our children spend more time at school than they do at home. We have to make sure that the phrase 'not my business' is something we find totally unacceptable. Education is not just about the three Rs; it is also about encouraging social responsibility and citizenship, caring for weaker people and just plain good manners. I see there is a sea change and some of the better schools and colleges and even universities are beginning to take far more pastoral care of those vulnerable people they have a duty to help bring up. So schools should not think, just because pupils have a 'get out of school card', i.e. a letter from parents saying they can leave school premises at lunchtimes, that it isn't their duty to ensure the kids behave responsibly in the community. And, actually, if the school knows there is a problem, they should override those parental wishes and keep them on the premises during school hours.

There was an AstroTurf pitch at this local school, and we asked them to open it later at night for kids to play football, but we were informed that neighbours would complain about the floodlights. We have so much publicly owned property that we just don't make available for community use. We should ask that they are kept open after hours. So much could happen to encourage children and young people to expand their horizons, improve their education and take up hobbies, especially sport, if we asked the community to volunteer to keep these places open.

Everybody then just passed the buck, time and time again. It seemed nobody wanted to come up with an innovative and fresh solution. Everyone wanted to stay in their box especially if it was a nine-to-five one. No wonder Garry was pacing the landing at night if he heard a noise outside. Even he began to wonder whether a move was the only option left. We were ordinary, decent, hard-working people who just wanted to be left in peace to bring up our family and enjoy our home and community. It wasn't a lot to ask. It did begin to feel like we were living in a medieval castle; we were under siege by an army of violent raiders but no one was coming to save us.

One evening, Garry went out to confront a gang of lads who were sitting on the bonnet of Zoe's boyfriend Tom's car. Garry went no further than the doorway and tried to be reasonable.

'Now, lads,' he said, 'would you mind moving off the bonnet, please. You're going to damage it.'

'Fuck off, you speccy-eyed fucker,' came the jeering response. 'Get in or we'll come and shag your wife.'

Garry didn't bat an eyelid and did a good job of pretending he didn't care. 'All right,' he said, 'have it your way. I'll just go in and call the police.'

Eventually the lads sloped off, muttering to themselves.

But the abuse went on. One afternoon, Garry was gardening out the front when he saw a lad urinating up a nearby fence.

'Oi!' he said. 'Do you mind? I've got teenage daughters here!'

'Fuck off,' was the drunken response and much worse – you can imagine the foul ranting.

We tried to shield our young daughters from the worst of all this, but our stress levels were soaring. We felt totally helpless and utterly abandoned by the authorities.

Garry wasn't alone in trying to tackle bad behaviour. Others would also come out if they heard a disturbance. I am going to protect their identities by not naming them. One evening, there was a terrible rumpus across the road and three neighbours came out to find a young lad aged about seventeen lying in one of the gardens. He'd been beaten up, pummelled so badly that at first they wondered if he was dead. Just as they were picking him up off the ground, along came his attacker for another go. But it wasn't another lad: he'd been beaten up by a girl of about 19. Luckily, the friends who were with her were trying to hold her back, but she was still trying to swing more punches. Garry swore later that she was high on drugs. She was extremely aggressive, swearing and cursing right in Garry's face, and it took three of her mates to pull her away. How she didn't punch him I'll never know. The police were called but, as usual, when they turned up, it was too late. The young lad staggered off with his face bloody and bruised, and everyone went back inside their homes, shaken up by what had happened. Amy and I were watching at the window. We all were terribly upset.

After Garry died, I got a letter from the lad's mother, laid on a single rose on my doorstep, thanking us for our efforts with her son that night.

> I'm so sorry to hear of your sad loss. I believe your husband/dad helped my son who was assaulted by the subway about three months ago. I am so grateful for that, and wished I had known who he was so that I could've thanked him.
>
> It is a terrible world that a grown man cannot protect his own property without being attacked by a gang of teenagers. No words can ease your pain at this time but I hope to God justice is done.

And so to the events of that night.

The next chapters of this book have been extraordinarily hard to write, not only because it meant reliving what happened but also because, six years on, my emotions and those of our daughters are still very raw and very real. The lady who wrote the letter above was right – no words can ease our pain, even the ones I have set down here. Only by campaigning for change, standing up for other victims and never ever letting authority, government or those in power forget us can I feel any sense of a terrible wrong somehow being put right. I am far from having what is termed 'closure'; Garry's killers will come out of prison one day and there will be a tremendous amount of soul-searching to go through when that day comes. Garry was murdered in cold blood in a quiet suburb for nothing more than looking out for others. As I describe in later chapters, I have tried to turn that senseless act into something positive, but it doesn't mean I am any less determined to make sure he didn't die for nothing. If this book achieves anything, it will be to demonstrate that the original anger and hurt and upset and grief, if channelled in the right way, can be used as a huge force for good.

I have met other victims of homicide and violent attacks that have left their loved ones as living dead. We all have to find our way through this dark tunnel to get out and survive. The injustice and the loss can eat you from the inside out. Some victims are utterly consumed by hatred and, to me, this means they too are being slowly killed. So the ones who stole the lives of their loved ones win again by destroying theirs too.

This will never happen to my family. We will fight for justice and for changes in the law, in policing and in society. In that way, we are working through our loss and devastation. Garry would want us to move on with our lives and to be happy. I believe he is watching over us still, but more of that later.

When Garry died, a part of me died too. But what was left has become far stronger, and something to be reckoned with. If Garry bequeathed a lasting legacy, that is it.

SIX

A Cruel and Random Act

Do you remember what you did last Friday night? If your family is anything like mine, the answer is 'nothing out of the ordinary'. A sigh of relief that work/college/school is over and the weekend is here again. A chance to recharge your batteries, and spend time on hobbies or with family and friends. Perhaps a couple of early drinks down the pub and a takeaway, an evening at the cinema, or just lazing around the TV in your 'sloggies'. For most people, it's the welcome end of the working week: a night for relaxing and doing nothing in particular. Housekeeping chores like washing, ironing and cleaning can wait until after the Saturday morning lie-in. Friday is 'me' time.

For the Newlove family, Friday, 10 August 2007 was one of those typical nights. Garry and I had been to work and the girls to school and college. Zoe was doing an evening shift at IKEA, like many college students supporting her social life and wardrobe with a part-time job. Danielle and Amy were in their bedrooms chilling and adding a fortune to their phone bills, talking for hours to friends they had just spent the day with. 'What more can they have to talk about?' Garry would ask. In an all-female house, with only Alfie the dog as a male supporter, he was hopelessly outnumbered. We would roll our eyes and not answer. I was as bad; it's a female thing and inexplicable to men. They just don't get it.

The girls were looking forward to watching the final of *Britain's Got Talent*. Garry was too, but it wasn't my thing at all. I hadn't felt well that day and, unusually for me, had left work early. Friday was one of the firm's busiest days of the week and I hated going off sick, but I had no choice. I felt queasy and had an upset stomach, so by early afternoon I was on the train home from Manchester.

I didn't even feel up to cooking that evening, so I certainly didn't want to watch a lot of loud music and excitement. Garry offered to cook me a 'chucky' (soft-boiled) egg and some toasted soldiers. He'd suggested Chinese takeaway for everyone but I didn't fancy it. However, I could definitely eat an egg, especially the way Garry made them. Around about 8 p.m., I went upstairs to bed. We had a TV in the bedroom, and I planned to watch *Midsomer Murders* – one of my favourites. I was the only one in the house who loved that programme, and I was teased unmercifully for it.

'Oh, Mum!' Garry, Danielle or Zoe would shout when it came on. 'There can't be many more people living in that village – they must all have been killed off by now!'

I always ignored their taunts. For me, the show had a good storyline and I quite liked the scenery too. So I was happy enough to retire early that night and watch my favourite programme in peace.

Garry and I were both stressed and had had a few niggly arguments that week; nothing serious, just the usual bickering caused by long hours at work and silly domestic stuff. We were more than ready for our summer holiday soon and were tired and tetchy. Both of us were stubborn and neither would apologise. But here he was, with his peace offering of delicious comfort food. How could I refuse?

He sat on the side of the bed and put his arms round me.

'We're going to have a fantastic holiday,' he said. 'I can't wait, can you?'

'Too right. Oh, Garry, I'm so looking forward to it. Two weeks off!'

The following week, we would all be flying to Lanzarote for a fortnight's break. Zoe was 18 now, and I wondered if it would be the last holiday we'd have as a family. This one was going to be very special.

We both said 'love you' and we kissed, and as we did Amy walked in.

'Euwwww!' she squealed in mock disgust, hiding her eyes. 'Get a room, will you!'

We laughed. 'Amy,' I said, 'I don't mean to be funny, but we are actually in our own bedroom here. Or hadn't you noticed?'

She rolled her eyes at us in that special way only 12 year olds can and laughed too.

'Come on, Amy,' Garry said. '*Talent*'s on in a minute and your Chinese is ready. Let's give your mum a bit of peace. She can't wait to see who Tom Barnaby is digging up this week.'

He winked at me by the bedroom door. 'I'll check on you in a bit. We're only teasing, you know.'

'I know,' I replied. 'Don't worry, I can take it. Go on – see you later.'

Garry padded downstairs. He wasn't wearing shoes or socks. It was a warm night and he had on a T-shirt and shorts. In a few days' time, that would be his day and evening wear. He loved the sun and going on holiday; it gave him the chance to let his hair down and enjoy partying and chatting to new people. He worked hard at his job, but his true passion was music and entertaining. His days as a DJ around Manchester's clubs had never really left him, even though he was 'suited and booted' now, always formally dressed in shirt, tie and cufflinks, in his role as a manager.

My programme started and I settled back into the pillow with a contented sigh. I'd had a long week and I wasn't feeling great, but at least I was heading for a nice break in the sun, and relaxation.

A minute or so later, I sat upright, my head turned to the door. I thought I could hear voices: the sound of shouting and raucous laughing. It wasn't coming from the bedroom TV, or from the living room where Garry and the girls were. The noises were getting louder and appeared to be coming closer. I groaned, not wanting to believe it. 'Here we go again,' I thought. 'Weekend gangs of teenagers walking through the subway.' Another weekend of crossing fingers that there would be no damage to our cars and those of the neighbours. Why couldn't they just clear off somewhere else?

Our neighbourhood was still being plagued by anti-social behaviour, and, despite fine words and lots of meetings, nothing had been done to tackle it. I remember saying to my neighbour as we walked home from one of the community liaison groups, 'We're just going round and round in circles. The same old faces saying the same old things. Nothing is being done to make this problem go away, and nothing will be done until someone is murdered.'

Little did I know how those words would come back to haunt me.

That Friday night, I heard the unmistakable sound of breaking glass. Amy heard it too and came in to tell me.

'I know, love,' I said. 'They're probably having a go at the digger.'

Our next-door neighbours were having their garden done at the time and a mini-digger had been left on their lawn ready for Monday morning. The wife, Amy, had a small baby and her husband worked away during the week. I was concerned as she was on her own with the baby.

We heard more shouting and laughing, followed by the unmistakable thud of a car door being kicked. I put my head in my hands. The passenger-side wing mirror of my car had already been damaged in a previous attack. Somebody – maybe me – would have a hefty repair bill in the morning. I couldn't take any more. Our Amy ran downstairs to see what was going on and I got out of bed.

'Garry!' I shouted from the landing. 'Could you just nip next door and see if she's OK? Oh, and can you check on my car? I thought I heard someone kicking it.'

Garry came out of the living room and looked up at me. 'Yeah, not a problem,' he said, walking barefoot down the hallway and out of the front door.

Those were the last words he ever spoke to me. No great farewell or 'I love you', just a simple, everyday response to a straightforward question – 'Yeah, not a problem.' Words that I now cherish.

Amy and Alfie, our little bichon frisé dog, trotted after Garry. After a few seconds, Danielle joined them. I learned later that as Garry walked out of the door, Zoe was just arriving home from work in her boyfriend Tom's car. All three girls, and Tom, would be eyewitnesses to the events about to unfold.

The laughter outside grew louder, followed by jeering and baying. It was a cold, cruel sound.

Then Amy tore up the stairs, two at a time, screaming her head off. 'Mum! Mum! Get dressed! Call an ambulance! Oh my God, call an ambulance!'

She was almost hysterical and I told her to calm down. Whatever was going on outside couldn't be that bad, could it?

'Mum,' she said, with growing panic in her voice, 'ring 999 now – please!'

Automatically I picked up the phone and dialled the number.

The woman at the other end asked me what service I wanted, and what the details of the incident were.

'I don't know,' I said, feeling slightly stupid. 'Something's gone wrong. I'm up Station Road North, Warrington. My daughter says someone's hurt. I don't know how bad it is, though. I'm really sorry – I should go and have a look, shouldn't I? Then I'll phone you back.'

I struggled to pull some joggers on over my pyjamas.

'Hurry up, Mum,' Amy shouted. 'You need to come down now. It's Dad – he's hurt!' She turned back.

I was still telling her to calm down as I came downstairs behind her. As I looked down, our next-door neighbour Amy was standing at the bottom of stairs with her baby in her arms. She was white-faced and shaking.

'Oh, Helen . . .' she began.

Our Amy had crashed to the floor at her feet. She'd collapsed. I screamed, rushing downstairs, despite the pain from an ankle injury I'd sustained a year before.

'Amy! Oh, God, Amy! What the hell's going on?'

Our neighbour Amy grabbed my arm as I knelt down by my daughter's side. 'Helen, leave her,' she shouted. 'I'll deal with her. Please – you need to get outside. You need to get to Garry . . . NOW!'

The look on her face made my heart pound and a sick feeling welled up in me as I hobbled out of the front door and down the driveway. All around me were voices telling me to hurry up. A knot of people had gathered just up the road. Someone was lying motionless on the ground. Oh, God, it couldn't be – no, it couldn't be. But it was.

'Garry! Garry! GAAARRRRYYY!!'

I screamed his name over and over again. Someone – I don't know who – stopped me in my tracks. His face was close to mine.

'Listen to me, Helen, listen to me,' he said, clutching both my arms. 'Just keep looking at me, OK? Just keep looking at me – he's going to be all right. He really is. Don't worry, love.'

The man was babbling his reassurance. I pushed him aside and carried on towards Garry. Now I felt like I was in slow motion, or sleepwalking. None of this was happening. Suddenly Zoe was in front of me.

'Mum, don't come near Dad,' she sobbed. 'Don't come near him.'

Tom, Zoe's boyfriend, was kneeling by Garry. He was frantically giving him mouth-to-mouth resuscitation, just like he'd been taught in his job as a personal trainer, and shouting down his mobile.

'There's no pulse!' he yelled.

I screamed again. 'Please, God, no! Don't take him away, please!'

Nausea overwhelmed me and I threw up over the nearest wall. Zoe cradled me in her arms, the tears streaming down her face.

'Mum, Dad will be OK,' she said, clinging to me. 'Don't worry, he'll be fine. I know it.'

What a girl. Now, when I think what she'd seen that night, I can only admire her courage and her protectiveness towards me.

Out of the darkness came flashing emergency lights. The paramedics jumped out of their vehicle and opened its back doors. People were being told to move back. There was shouting and chaos. Danielle was talking to one paramedic while the other two knelt over him. Another courageous young girl, trying to keep calm and level-headed as horror whirled all around her.

Garry was lifted into the ambulance on a stretcher. I pushed forward and stood on the first step. No one but me could take this journey with Garry. But I was to go no further.

'I'm sorry,' said one of the paramedics, 'but you can't come in. We have to get on with it. I'm really sorry.'

The doors were shut in my face.

'Please don't hurt him!' I screamed. 'He's had cancer. He has no stomach or spleen. Please be gentle with him!'

My words rushed away in a flash of lights and loud sirens that disappeared round the corner, taking my husband away from the home and family he loved. Our lives would never be the same again.

SEVEN

A Light Goes Out

As the ambulance rushed Garry to the hospital, I slumped onto the kerb. A glass of water was pressed into my hand and I could feel arms around my shoulders. I had to phone people – relatives, friends, anyone who could help. I rang my mum, who lived close by. My dad was in a nursing home by this time, and she wasn't used to taking late-night phone calls. But I needed to speak to her. When she answered, I told her Garry was injured and that I was scared. I can't remember her reply, but I knew I would see her as soon as she could make it. Then I phoned my best friend, Tina. She lived in Buxton, about 90 minutes away from Warrington.

'I'm coming now,' she said without hesitation. 'Where will you be?'

'I don't know,' I replied. 'Warrington General, I suppose . . . oh, please hurry up, Tina, I don't know what's going on.'

I tried ringing Garry's brother, Keith, who lives in Spain. I tried and tried to contact him but there was no reply. I was shouting hysterically into the phone, willing someone to answer. But I was howling into silence. It was no good my sitting there, going crazy. I had to do something.

'I need to go to the hospital,' I said, taking deep gulps of air. 'I need to go now.'

Tom took my hand. 'I'll take you, Helen,' he said. 'It's OK. I can drive. I can do it.'

Bless him. He adored Garry and would have done anything for him. He'd just tried to save his life. Now he was offering to take me to the hospital. He must've been so shocked and shaken up, but he was prepared to do this thing for all of us. We dashed over to his car, parked on our neighbour's driveway. As we drew near, a police officer stopped us.

'I'm sorry,' he said, 'but it's going to be difficult to get the car out of the drive. This is a crime scene now, I'm afraid.'

I couldn't believe what I was hearing. My husband had been brutally beaten up and I needed to be by his side.

'You've got to be kidding!' I roared. 'My husband could be dying and you're telling me I have to wait? I don't bloody believe this!'

The police officer looked ashamed. It wasn't his fault – he was only doing his job. But it was officialdom, and I would have to deal with a lot more of it in the weeks and months ahead.

'OK, I'll have to get permission,' he said.

It seemed like ages before word came through that we could take the car, but it was probably just minutes. However, it felt like the longest minutes of my life. All I could imagine was Garry lying in the back of that ambulance, his life slipping away while I stood uselessly on the pavement.

I don't know how we got to Warrington General Hospital without getting injured ourselves. I can hardly remember the journey. I just kept saying to Tom, 'He's dead, I know it. Garry's gone and I wasn't there for him.' Tom must have been in pieces, but he got us there and we rushed straight into A&E. (The impact of the name of the department still leaves me cold to this day and it was two years before I could even enter that hospital again.) We were told to take a seat. Garry had just arrived, they were working on him and there was no news yet.

My mouth was dry with fear and anxiety. I needed a glass of water desperately, but there was no water available, not even in the vending machines. It seems ridiculous to think it now, but I could feel myself getting furious at the lack of water. I didn't want Coca-Cola or Sprite or Fanta. I felt angry enough to smash one of those machines with my bare hands. Now I know it was suppressed rage combined with shock at what had happened. But just one glass of water would've been nice.

My mum arrived soon after and I collapsed, sobbing, into her arms.

'I'm sorry, Mum,' I wept. 'This is the last thing you need.'

She hugged me tight, as tight as she could considering her own frailty. 'I'm here, love,' she whispered. 'I'm here now.'

We sat in the waiting area for about 15 minutes, just crying and holding on to each other. There were so many other people in there that warm Friday night. I hardly noticed them, but each would have had his or her own story to tell. I couldn't believe I was living through this one, a story I had never dreamed of and could barely comprehend was true.

I needed some fresh air and so I went outside, just as my best friend Tina rushed in. She'd been at a works party and left immediately to get to me. That's what having a best friend is truly about. She put her arms around me, saying she couldn't believe this was happening. I knew the feeling.

I'm very glad she was there, because at that moment a nurse arrived, saying the doctor wanted to speak with me. 'Can we just go over into this room?' she said, pointing to a door marked 'Family'. 'We'll have a lot more privacy in there.'

'Oh no,' I replied, starting to panic, 'there's no way I'm going in there with you. I watch *Casualty*. I know what happens in those rooms.'

It sounded daft, talking about a TV drama when all this was going on in real life, but I meant it. Every time someone gets taken into a hospital's family room on that show, it only means one thing – the worst news possible. I didn't want to hear what I was sure they were going to tell me, and it took the combined efforts of Mum, Tina and Tom to get me in there.

'It's OK,' they urged. 'Let's just listen to what he has to say. We're here for you.'

But it wasn't OK. The doctor came in and tried to give me Garry's jewellery: a gold chain and his rings.

I wouldn't take them. 'You can put them back on him right now,' I said, pushing his hand away, outraged and scared. What did this mean?

'No, Helen,' the doctor said gently, obviously guessing I was thinking Garry had no further need for these cherished possessions. 'It's only because we've had to put a neck collar on him. That's all.'

'How is he?' My voice was quavering, half of me not wanting to hear the answer.

There was a pause and the doctor looked uneasy. 'He's very poorly, Helen,' he said. 'His heart stopped in the ambulance. That's why they couldn't let you in. But they worked on him and he came back. I have to tell you that one of his pupils is dilated and he's in a coma.'

'Is that medically induced?' I asked. God knows where that came from. Probably *Casualty* again.

'I'm afraid not,' said the doctor. 'His brain is haemorrhaging very badly and he hasn't woken up. We need to carry out some scans immediately.'

'Can I see him first?'

He said he'd have to seek permission, but, after a few minutes' wait, it was granted and with Mum by my side I went in to see my poor husband.

What they'd done to him was almost indescribable. His face was swollen and bloody and there was a footprint clearly stamped into his forehead. His hands were bruised from where he had tried to protect himself against the blows. There was a brace around his neck and – unknown to me at this time – he had suffered more than 40 internal injuries. How could anyone have inflicted so much cruelty on one person in such a short space of time? I wanted more than anything to hold him, protect him, but he was so poorly I wasn't allowed to touch him. Then we were told we had to go, as he needed to be moved for the scan. We were only there for seconds and we went out of the room sobbing.

Thankfully, we were met by my sister Marie, who had just arrived. She is a theatre sister at a hospital in Manchester and, like me, is a very no-nonsense person. First of all, she insisted that I have a glass of water and actually went to fetch it herself. She wouldn't take no for an answer. She sat and waited with us. Thank God she was by my side when the consultant entered the family room. I knew by his face that I wasn't going to get good news.

'Garry is very poorly indeed,' he said, echoing the words of the doctor. 'When we moved him for the MRI scan, it was touch and go in the lift. However, we've managed to do the scans and we've faxed them over to a specialist in Liverpool. I'm sorry to say the results showed that his injuries are too severe to transfer him to that unit. All we can do is wait and see.'

I turned to our Marie. 'Tell me what all this means,' I said. 'I'll only take it from you.'

As gently as she could, Marie explained the brutal facts of severe head injury. It was terrible news to have to swallow. Basically, Garry's brain was swelling and flooded by blood and there was no room for it to expand in his rigid skull. As it continued to press against this hard bone, the soft tissue was dying. As well as the direct injuries, the more severe the trauma in the brain, the more irreversible the damage would be.

'The consultant's right,' she said. 'All we can do is wait and see. Mum, you really should go home and get some rest. I'll stay the night with our Helen.'

So that's just what she did, right through that terrible night as I swung from hope to despair and back again. I prayed like I had when I thought I'd lose him from cancer, making the same deals with God. Garry was moved into a recovery side ward as there were no beds available in the intensive care unit that night. I was allowed to be with him. I kissed his face tenderly and stroked his cheek, telling him that I wouldn't leave him.

'You beat cancer, Garry,' I whispered to him, 'and the odds were against you then, too. I know you can survive this. The girls need you, Garry. Come on, wake up, love. You're scaring me.'

I talked and talked to him the whole night as the nurses came in silently to check on him. I tried to read their expressions but they were closed. It was the longest, blackest night of my life and I thought it would never end.

Then, in the morning, I found hope. As I sat by his side, I noticed that he was breathing on his own, against the ventilator. I was overjoyed. Surely this was something good? I called over the doctor, who said he'd have a word with the consultant. I tried to get Marie excited about it, but she remained calm.

'Let's just wait and see,' she said, clasping my hand.

I got quite angry that she wasn't as happy as I was. Now I know that her medical background was telling her what it really meant.

Later that morning, the consultant came by. Straight away, I told him about Garry's breathing.

He sat by me and smiled a sad smile. 'You know, the brain is a very clever organ,' he said. 'I have to say that Garry's life is hanging by a thread and his brain is reacting to that. If he does survive, it is highly likely he will be in a persistent vegetative state. We will be doing further tests, but I have to say to you now, Helen, that you may have to decide whether the life-support machine should be turned off.'

As calm and as lovely as he was, his words destroyed any hope I had left. So now it was a matter of 'when', not 'if'.

'I think that you should go home to your girls,' he said gently, 'and perhaps try to rest.'

'No way,' I said, grabbing Marie's hand even tighter. 'I'm not going. I know what will happen. The minute I go, so will Garry. I won't be here for him. I'm not doing it.'

My breathing was shortening and I was on the verge of a panic attack. Marie made me look her right in the eye.

'The doctor's right, Helen,' she said. 'Those girls need you. They must've been up all night wondering what the hell's going on. You need to be with them.'

Oh, God, how could I find the words to tell them what had happened these last few hours? What could I say that would make them feel any better? I tried to calm down and think rationally. The last memory of their father was of a battered and bloodied man lying on a dirty road. Was that how they'd want to remember him? Or did I need to go home and tell them he was being treated with care and dignity?

In the end, there was no choice. An hour or so later I was at home, the girls crowding round me for news. They looked so tired, having been up all night giving witness statements and worrying about their dad. We sat in the living room and held hands. I wanted to cry but I needed to be strong. They needed hope just as much as I did. I told them their dad was very poorly and asleep, but that he was being well looked after. They wanted to know if they could come back to the hospital with me right there and then. I said I needed a shower and some time to think.

In truth, I'd already made up my mind. Garry was too ill and in too much of a mess for them to see him at that stage. If, by a miracle, he started to get better, that would be the time. If not . . . well, I couldn't think about 'if not'. Not at the moment. I took a shower and cried hard behind the locked door. I let the water run for ages, muffling the sound of my sobs so they couldn't hear me. When I came back down, Tina had arrived and I was itching to get back. Much as I didn't want to leave them, I had to be by Garry's side. My mum was also here now and she would take good care of them. I kissed them all and promised I would pass on their kisses and hugs to their dad.

As I walked down the drive to Tina's car, Amy came tearing after us, a piece of paper in her hand.

'Mum! Mum! Wait! I've written this for Dad. It's a letter. Will you read it to him?'

My heart almost broke as I took the sheet of lined A4 paper, torn from an exercise book, out of her hand.

''Course I will, love,' I said, hugging her tight and trying not to break down. 'He'll appreciate that. Thank you.'

I shoved the letter in my bag and got into the car. 'God help those poor children,' I thought. It was so hard to leave them like this.

When we arrived at the hospital, we found out from the ward sister that Garry had been moved into intensive care, but during the move he'd taken a turn for the worse. His other pupil was now dilated. It was now time, she said, to consider bringing in the children or taking a photograph for them to see if they couldn't face visiting.

I felt the weight of everything crushing down on me. I'd only been home for a shower and all this had happened. I couldn't stand there and coolly take a photograph of my dying husband. It just felt too weird. That said, I wanted to protect the girls, not frighten them. Yet they had a right to say goodbye to their father, if that's what had to happen. My head was in bits, but my heart told me they had to be consulted and given the choice. Not to do so would be totally wrong for such a close family as ours. I would never forgive myself, and I knew neither would they.

I was taken to see Garry in the unit. Ironically, it was the exact same place he'd been in as he battled against stomach cancer. He was only 32 then but he'd fought hard and come through it. This time I felt our luck was ebbing away. I couldn't believe he was fighting for his life again in the very same spot. It was so, so cruel. I rooted in my bag for a tissue to wipe away the tears that were now flowing freely. Then I spotted Amy's folded-up letter.

They say the hearing is the last thing to go, so, taking a deep breath and praying that I could have strength to get me through the following few minutes, I unfolded the letter and began to read.

To Daddy,

I am unable to see you right now as you are too ill but I know you can fight this as you are a strong, loving man who I know loves me no matter what. I am asking you to be strong and don't give in as I love you too much to believe that you won't go without a fight. I had a dream last night that you woke up and you were fine, except you didn't know me at all! I would still try to help you remember. I will stick by you while you are in hospital and I will take care of Mummy. I can't get across to you how much I will miss you and I don't know what I would do without you. You have always been there for me when I am down and you always put a smile on my face (even if it is a rubbish joke). You mean the world to me and I wouldn't change you for the world. When you get out of here I will be there with a big smile on my face. I hope you can hear me right now as I hope it will give you more strength and determination to wake up. I thought I saw Nana Newlove's face in the TV last night and I keep seeing her. I know she is here with you looking out for you and is probably offering cornflakes or Thornton's toffee. I love you with all my heart so please don't give in. We are taking care of you and Mummy.

We will deeply miss you and I want you to know you are the best dad anyone can ask for. I love you so much and I do hope you can fight this. I love you! From your darling daughter . . . who loves you so much and from the whole family! WE LOVE YOU!! AND DON'T GIVE IN!! XXXXOOOOXXX.

By the time I'd come to the end of that heartbreaking letter from a daughter to her beloved dad, a letter that poured out all the love a 12 year old can give, I'd made up my mind. I would go home, get the girls and bring them to see their father for the last time.

As I was leaving, Garry's brother, Keith, arrived with his sons, Jarrod and Glynn. Keith had been delayed by heavy storms in Spain but had finally made it. He looked devastated. Garry idolised his big brother and they were so close.

When I got home, the girls looked so tired and lost. I sat with them and explained that Dad was worse, but that the doctors were looking after him very well and that they told me to ask if the girls wanted to come in and see how he was. But I also told them if they didn't want to come that was perfectly fine. I did not want to pressurise them after all they had gone – and were going – through. Our home had people coming in and out, asking questions about this and that. I think over all of this now and I really do not know how they held themselves together. All they wanted was to have their dad back. They did not hesitate and they all said that they wanted to see him. We never spoke a word on that journey to the hospital. There was simply nothing to say, so we sat in silence, wrapped up in our own thoughts.

We arrived at the intensive care unit and I told the nurse that they wanted to go in to see their dad. She explained to the girls what they would see when they entered the unit and, although it felt and looked frightening, it would be OK. 'The machines make it look a lot worse than it is with all the noises and tubes,' she said, 'but it is fine.'

I asked the other family members to stay in the waiting room as I didn't want the girls to feel any more overwhelmed than they already felt. So, along with the nurse, we walked over to Garry and stood around his bedside in the ICU. Watching the girls look at their dad was unbearable. I told them to talk to him and I told Garry that his daughters and Tom were here to see him. Danielle just broke her heart on the spot. Amy stared and cried. Zoe – well, she was old enough to know exactly what was going on. She found it difficult to show any tears but she was angry; angry that he was lying there and that nothing appeared to be happening. She stormed out of the unit, too emotional to take any more in.

'Why isn't he opening his eyes?' Amy demanded. 'Why isn't anyone doing anything? What's going on?'

Typical Amy, so young, but already headstrong and questioning – just like her mum. I told her that Dad was on special medication and that he had to rest, but he could hear what people were saying and that she should talk to him about the letter she'd written.

I told all the girls if they wanted to give Dad lots of cuddles and kisses they could, as he could hear them. But he looked too scary for them. They were so shell-shocked, not only by what had happened but also by Garry's appearance and the bank of machinery around him. Amy asked if I had read her letter to Dad and I told her I had. I said he'd heard every word that she had written down and that Dad would be proud of her.

Finally, it was time for them to leave. The girls wanted to stay with me, but I wouldn't allow it. I didn't want them to go through what I was about to face during the darkest of nights ahead. They'd been through enough and, besides, I told them there simply wasn't the space for them on the ward. The doctors would not allow it as the nurses had to do their job through the night and with all the machines it would not be appropriate. So they said their goodbyes in turn and as they did I could feel my heart wanting to tear itself from my body. I was angry and exhausted, and I felt like I was going mad.

Keith, Marie and I took turns to sit by Garry's bed. A camp bed had been put up in the family room in case we wanted to sleep. In my case, I didn't think there was much chance of that, but I appreciated the gesture and eventually I did fall asleep for a short while. But not before I spent hours talking to Garry about our life together. I covered so many subjects – our courtship and wedding, his DJ-ing adventures, the birth of our girls, the holidays we'd had, the trivial fall-outs and make-ups. I told him everything, and I even told him that his mother, who passed away in 2000, wasn't going to have him before I did. 'So, if she is with you, do not turn to her and leave us all alone here,' I whispered. And all the time, all through the night, there was the beep-beep, blip-blip of the machinery keeping Garry alive. It's a noise I can still hear in my head now, and I have to close my eyes to make it go away.

Occasionally, the nurses came in to check on Garry. 'Is there any change?' I asked hopefully.

'No, love,' they replied. 'Sorry . . .' They found it hard to meet my eyes.

I finally slept, and woke up at around 6 a.m. on Sunday, 12

August. The horror and pain rushed straight towards me as I opened my eyes, and I knew I had a huge decision to make. I felt I couldn't go through with it. I leaned on Keith's shoulder and said, 'I really cannot do this,' and broke down. Time was ticking. Soon I knew I would be called in to see the consultant.

As well as Marie, Keith and me going into the consultant's office, there was a police officer in attendance. However, I never really took in what that person represented. I just wanted to focus on hearing that Garry had awoken from his coma and things would be getting back to normal or as normal as it possibly could be. So we all sat down in his office and he started talking very matter-of-factly. I can remember him speaking but I wasn't taking anything in until he raised the subject of organ donation. Equally clearly I remember replying that Garry always said he'd had enough taken out of him during the treatment for cancer. He never wanted to lose any more, and I would stand by his wishes.

The consultant nodded, then spoke again. 'Unfortunately, it's not a decision for us to consider anyway, right now,' he said, 'because it's now likely to involve the Coroner.'

'What? How do you mean? What's the Coroner got to do with any of this? My husband isn't dead yet, for God's sake!'

'All the tests show us that Garry isn't responding,' he replied, 'and the next stage is for independent brain tests to be carried out. I'm so sorry, but we can do no more than that. If these tests tell us there is no brain activity, then I'm afraid we have to inform the Coroner, as it then could be a murder investigation.'

His words hardly registered. All I was worried about was whether the tests would hurt Garry, but I was told they wouldn't. Two doctors would carry them out and the results would be available almost immediately afterwards. The consultant would have a look over the results and then speak to the family.

'We will, of course, respect your wishes if you would like Garry to receive the Last Rites,' the consultant added.

Of course I did. I knew his mother would come back to haunt me if I didn't. Silly thought, I suppose, but at that moment it felt very real. I wanted to make Garry's passing as good as it could be, and to hand him to God in the best way.

He suggested that if there were other family members who wanted to see Garry then it would be better to get in touch now rather than later as he would be carrying out the tests within the next hour.

The chaplain was sent for and, while we waited, more relatives gathered in the family room. When the chaplain arrived, he took a quick look at Garry and walked straight out again. We were astonished – what was he playing at? Then he came back in and apologised to us all.

'I'm sorry,' he said, 'but when I saw how badly beaten that poor man was I was so angry I had to walk out.'

And that from a man of the cloth. It was clear, even at this terrible moment, that what had happened less than 48 hours earlier would touch many, many people.

Garry was given the Last Rites. Then it was time for the tests. I couldn't face watching the doctors do their work, so Marie and Keith went in. I begged Marie to make sure they wouldn't hurt Garry and she promised me she would. The rest of us sat and waited. Sitting and waiting was all we had seemed to do in the last two days. Only 48 hours but they seemed an eternity.

As expected, the tests showed there was no reflex at all, and that Garry was being kept alive by the machine only. It was my decision, and mine alone, to take the next step. The sick feeling in the pit of my stomach will stay with me forever. Questions were racing through my head – could he be alive? Had they got it wrong? If we left him, might he just wake up? How could I do this to him?

The ICU team sat with me and explained, as tactfully as they could, that there was nothing to suggest Garry would pull through. Severe haemorrhaging had made it impossible. All hope was gone.

We took turns to say goodbye to Garry. When it was my turn, I told him I loved him dearly and that he was the best husband, father and friend anyone could wish for. I told him I would make him proud of the way his daughters would live their lives.

'There's one more thing,' I whispered to him. 'Let me know you're still around. I know you laughed at me, but please send me a white feather to say you are still around and looking after us. If you see your mum, say hello and give her my love. I wish you peace, my darling. You have suffered enough. Now I'm going to let you go.'

Then all the family stood around Garry and I was asked if I was ready. I nodded my assent. I lay over Garry's body, wrapping my arms tightly around his chest.

'Are you ready, Helen?' someone asked.

Then the click. Garry's chest rose and fell once more, and for the last time. Then he lay silent.

I screamed and screamed, clinging to him like a drowning man clings to a rock.

'Oh, God, oh, God, please . . . no! Please don't take him away! Please . . .!'

It took several hands to peel me off Garry's body, and to support me as we staggered back to the family room. He'd gone. My lovely, funny, warm-hearted, generous Garry had gone. I couldn't take it in and kept asking everyone if he was really, really dead. Their silence spoke volumes. We looked at each other blankly, then we lost control and broke down.

The nurse in charge tapped on the door of the family room. 'Garry's heart has now stopped,' he said.

I looked at my sister and asked her what that meant and she

told me that when the machine is turned off, the heart still beats for a short while and they have to inform you of that. Oh my God, how much more? My own heart was breaking down too.

Outside the family room, the police officers assigned to the incident were talking to one another, their faces taut and serious. Garry was wheeled out of that room in a metal box. My husband was no longer my husband. He was no longer the girls' father. He was now Man A, the victim at the heart of a murder investigation.

EIGHT

Shattered Lives

Garry was dead. No more would we see him, hear him or feel him. He was gone forever.

When we stopped crying for a moment, our Marie wiped her eyes with a tissue and looked at me squarely in the face, a question in her eyes.

'I know what you're going to say,' I said, 'and I've already thought about it. Only I can do it, Marie. I'm their mum, and it has to be me.'

She nodded. Who else but me could break such terrible news to three young girls? News that would shatter their lives, destroy and tear apart their happy childhood. News that was final and irreversible. News that their adored father was no longer there for them.

I was so dazed that, to this day, I don't know how we got home. I don't even know who drove us. Perhaps it was the police. They certainly came with us, perhaps following behind, because they kept a respectful distance as I went in to deliver the news. Garry's brother and sister came with us, too. As I went through the front door, I saw my mum. Mums always know the truth, and when she saw my crumpled face she folded up and broke down. She loved Garry dearly and stared at me in disbelief.

The girls were still in the lounge. Marie took Mum into the kitchen with the rest of the family while I closed the door to speak to my three brave daughters. 'Deep breath and don't break down now, Helen,' I told myself. 'Be strong, you can do this.' The pain was horrendous and stays with me to this day.

I'd been up all night and just watched their father die. I must've looked horrendous. We sat down on the sofa and all three looked at me with expectancy and fear. The hope in their faces broke me up. Mum would kiss and make it better, Mum would make this horrible, horrible day go away, turn back the clock so we could just forget it, and Dad would come through the door laughing that we'd fallen for yet another of his silly pranks. 'Gotcha!'

I held them close to me and started very carefully and slowly saying the words I'd practised over and over again on the way home from the hospital. 'Dad was really poorly through the night,' I said, hardly daring to look at their little faces. 'Sadly, Dad has gone to sleep and has passed away. Dad has died.'

There was a moment's pause while they took in the awful news, then they just sobbed their hearts out. I grabbed them and held them close to me. Without a word, Zoe got up and walked out of the room and ran upstairs. Our Zoe's not a crier, and would deal with it in her own way. Like an anonymous letter-writer would say a few days later, no words could make up for their loss, and I didn't try. I couldn't believe that in the space of just 48 hours a huge hole had been blasted in our lives by an unspeakably cruel and random act. We clung on to each other like survivors from a shipwreck, crying and sobbing in our collective grief. Finally, exhausted from sleeplessness and my non-stop tears, I pulled away from them and dragged myself upstairs, leaning heavily on the handrail to support myself.

There was no noise from Zoe's room. Downstairs, I heard the low, muted voices of Garry's siblings and my sister doing their best to console Danielle and Amy. I lay on our bed, the bed I hadn't been in since Friday night. I buried my face in Garry's discarded T-shirt, the one he wore to bed most nights, breathing in his familiar smell, and howled. I grabbed our pillows. I needed to smell him. He was still with us, he had not died, he was still alive if I could smell him. God, please bring him back . . .

The next few hours were a blur. Garry's brother and sister eventually left, as did my mum, who needed to get home. Our Marie stayed, trying to be our rock. The house seemed to be full of people, and yet strangely empty. There had been a seismic shift, an earthquake that had made us victims. The police understood this, and were trying to do their jobs, while remaining sensitive to what had just happened to us. As the girls were the primary witnesses, officers were already interviewing them for statements while their memories were still sharp. I didn't know it at the time, but that process had already started as I sat by Garry's bed. Perhaps fearing the worst, or at least preparing for a charge of grievous bodily harm had Garry survived, the police had taken statements from the girls and taken their clothes away for forensic examination.

There was, as I was about to find out, a good reason for this frantic activity by the police. They already had some people in custody, suspected of involvement in the crime. The police had told me on the Saturday afternoon after the attack on Garry that they had arrested nine people 'but they may not all have been involved'. I did not care at that time. Garry was my priority. Now it transpired that five youths were to be charged. Some of these had been picked up on the Friday of the murder; more of them on the Saturday. Another of them, a lad called Adam Swellings, was picked up on the Monday. The speed with which the arrests were made suggested these lads all knew one another very well. And presumably so did the police.

Once the police had them in custody, it was vital that those suspected of the greatest involvement were identified immediately. Despite their grief, my girls had to perform this task at an identity parade. Brave girls, they had no hesitation in taking part, but during the parade, at Stockton Heath police station in Warrington, our Marie (who accompanied them) was told she shouldn't be in the same room as the girls for the duration of the parade, because the lads' solicitors objected on the grounds she might 'coach' the girls. So she had to turn and face the wall while it was carried out. She felt as if she'd been the one in trouble and had been sent to the naughty corner. It was very demeaning for her, but she insisted that she was staying with the girls and would not leave. Our emotions were running high and the girls were the ones who needed all the help and support we could give them to get through all these stages. To think they had never been in trouble all their young lives and would have been petrified if they'd brought trouble to us. Now they were being thrust into the criminal justice system to fight for justice for their dad, while grieving at the same time. Although I didn't know it then, this would be my first experience of just how far the justice system is deeply biased towards the rights of the defendant. My girls were in bits, but they weren't allowed to be close to their aunty while they underwent such a traumatic experience. Remember they were only 18, 15 and 12 at the time. It was only the first of the many such indignities that victims have to face routinely.

That night, I couldn't sleep and felt I was on autopilot. Amy slept in our bed because she was so worried about me. My sister was so concerned that she called our GP, who came out and prescribed me a month's worth of sleeping tablets, but they didn't seem to do much good. I would pass out for a few hours and wake up, wondering what there was to wake up for. I'd doze briefly but then open my eyes feeling like I hadn't slept at all.

The police were constantly around with questions, questions, questions. I had some of my own, not least when Garry's body could be released from the mortuary. I was horrified to learn that it could be three months at least before we could get him back.

'I'm sorry, Helen,' said our family liaison officer, 'but it's a murder investigation. It will take time.' But she said that she had to let us know that it was not as simple a procedure as they would like it to be.

I could only guess that the involvement of a gang meant the case would be more complex than if there was a single attacker. At that time, I was more concerned with giving my husband the tender, loving farewell he deserved and to lay him to rest in peace than I was with finding the evil people who had done this to him. That would come later.

However, the wheels were moving quickly. Five lads – Adam Swellings, Stephen Sorton and Jordan Cunliffe, plus two others who cannot be named for legal reasons – were charged with Garry's murder. The names were unfamiliar to me at that stage. I assumed they were local boys who knew the area, and that they were part of the wider gang who'd caused so much trouble around Fearnhead over the previous couple of years.

They appeared at Warrington Magistrates' Court for a preliminary hearing. I didn't attend, but Garry's brother, Keith, went along with some other family members. They came back absolutely gobsmacked at the sight of the five scrawny adolescents in the dock. 'How could kids who looked like that possibly do what they did to our Garry?' Keith said. Of course, one-to-one in a fair fight Garry would have seen them off with one arm tied behind his back, but against a feral hunting pack he stood no chance. The youths were remanded in custody pending further investigation and appearances at a later date, but it was the order of the judge in the case that proceedings move quickly.

Meanwhile, the press was gathering in force outside our house. Garry's murder and the way it had been carried out touched a collective public nerve and the story was being covered heavily in the national press and on TV. Journalists were constantly pestering the police press office for interviews. Not wanting to read anything about Garry's death, I had no idea at all of the interest that was building in the case, nor of the public outrage. I just wanted everyone to go away and leave us alone and for Garry to come back home, alive and well, as though it had all been a bad dream. I felt like the world had become a merry-go-round, yet I had not moved a muscle, just sitting in one spot wanting my life to go back to normal.

Obviously, that wasn't going to happen. The best course of action was to follow the family liaison officer's advice and give the press something quickly, which would hopefully take the heat off. I have to say that, although they were all down the road, photographers and TV people included, they were being very respectful towards us. So I arranged for them to have a photograph of Garry and the letter that Amy wrote to him as he lay in hospital. That, I hoped, would do the trick.

The emotion of that letter, written by an innocent 12 year old to her beloved father, struck a deep chord and only served to fuel the outrage that many people up and down the UK felt about what had happened. Within a day or so, we began to receive letters, hundreds of them, mostly from strangers who wanted to express their shock and sympathy at Garry's death. I read a few at the time but being constantly reminded of the murder was terribly hard, and I put most of them aside to read at a later date, which I did. Below are just a selection of quotes from the many we received:

Just to let you know that we are thinking and praying for you at this difficult time.

It is time for the government to act and to listen to the people who elect them to look after the good law-abiding people of this country.

The world has gone mad and this country is no longer a decent place to live. My in-laws live in France now, and say they left because law and order has broken down. In a few years' time we will be joining them for a better way of life.

I'm 65 years old and, like millions of other people, I want to see the return of the death penalty and radically harsh punishments for such thuggery.

What came across strongly in these letters was the anger that this should have happened at all in a civilised country, least of all to someone like Garry. Drunken gang attacks happened to other people in inner cities; people now saw how easily it could have been them, in any village, town or street. They were obviously sick and tired of yobbery going unpunished because the system was too ineffective to do anything about it. At that time, we had had years of apologies for unacceptable behaviour, including broken homes, lack of education, jobs, poverty, etc. Social workers ruled, and the politicians of the time were listening and disregarding the few brave voices who tried to speak up. One obvious example is the relaxation of licensing hours to turn us into a continental 'café culture'. Any fool could see the outcome – the rise in alcohol-related anti-social behaviour and the growth of the final bill to the NHS paid for by the public purse.

Although I didn't – and couldn't – take it in at the time, Garry's murder was already beginning to provide a platform for decent, hard-working people in this country to have their say. What I read at the time gave me comfort, just knowing there were people out there who felt the same sense of shock and injustice as we did, and I would like to thank everyone who took the trouble to write to me during those dark, dark days. Your thoughts and sentiments were much appreciated. Those kind words from strangers who shared our pain were the life raft we clung to through the storm that engulfed us. Your compassion and understanding kept us afloat and reassured us it was still a good world with good people in it. We had collided with another universe that night, one dark and evil, but it was not bigger than the one we inhabited.

We were now officially 'victims of crime', at least according to the leaflet we'd been given by Victim Support. It was like a manual for victims and, while the police meant well in passing it on to us, I didn't want to read a word of it. It seemed very formulaic, telling us what we should and shouldn't be feeling. How can anyone say what's right or wrong in any situation? To me, it looked exhausting and my on-going sleep problems meant that I couldn't take in very much anyway.

I certainly didn't want to leave the house, that much was certain. The week after Garry's death was marked by a candlelit vigil attended by people from all over the neighbourhood. The girls and I didn't go. We couldn't face a public appearance, not yet. There was a collection and many expressions of support from those who attended, who included our Marie and Keith.

However, not everyone was happy and supportive. When flowers were laid close to the spot where Garry died, an old woman living nearby complained that they were on her wall. I couldn't believe it when I heard that, but I was in no state to find out why she objected. I told my mum that it wasn't worth getting upset about it and asked her to move them to one side if it made the lady feel better. It was the very least of my worries.

After three weeks, our family liaison officer told me that Garry's body was finally ready for release and burial. She was always so sensible and sensitive with us, and she knew this would be a particularly painful moment for us as a family.

'Did you want to visit Garry one final time before he is released?' she asked.

'I don't know,' I replied. 'It's hard to decide. What do you think?'

'Well,' she said as carefully as she could, 'if you decide yes, then do it sooner rather than later. I have to tell you, Helen, that he isn't in a great way.'

I didn't understand what she meant, and asked her to explain. What she told me, as diplomatically but as straightforwardly as she could, was that Garry's body had undergone five different autopsies, as requested by each of the defendants' lawyers, which she explained was the defence's right to do. That crucified me. How dare they do that without asking my permission? What possible extra information could be gained by doing the autopsy over and over again – *four* more times – that the first autopsy had not produced? I understand that it is just routine procedure but it is one that has to change. I often wonder if these defence lawyers would be as thoughtless with their demands if it was their spouse or child being cut up and sewn back together again and again like a piece of meat on a butcher's block. How do they sleep at night? I was so upset and angry because Garry always said that, after his death, he didn't want to be an organ donor. 'I've been cut open enough,' he said, referring to his cancer operation. 'I don't want to go through that again, dead or alive.'

Needless to say, I didn't go to see Garry, and neither did Keith. The memories of him lying in the hospital, battered and bruised almost beyond recognition, were bad enough. Yet I feel guilty now that I didn't.

Even though Garry's body could be released, I learned that it would be without his brain. Forensic tests were still being carried out on it. Sickened as I was to hear that, I decided to wait for a short while longer while the tests were completed and the brain put back into his skull. I wanted to make sure those tests were done properly, as they might provide crucial evidence in a forthcoming trial. More than that, though, I wanted him back in one piece. Garry's brain was a good one – sharp, witty, intelligent and full of fun. It deserved to be with his body on its final journey.

NINE

A Final Farewell

Now we had received confirmation that Garry's body could be released, we had a funeral to organise. When I say 'we', I mean that it was mostly Marie, Keith and the rest of the family. Getting the wheels in motion was something that was far beyond me at that stage, though I did pick the colour of the coffin and the flowers. I could hardly believe I was doing it; very often I thought I might just wake myself up out of this living nightmare and see Garry standing next to me once again.

The funeral directors that we contacted were a local family business called Knox & Son Ltd. Harry was our coordinator and, I have to say, a perfect gentleman. So kind, warm and supportive. Now, I know people might say, 'Well, that's what they are paid to do,' but I personally want to thank Harry and the company. At all stages of the process, Harry was just kindness itself. Obviously, they'd heard what had happened and were as shocked as anyone about Garry's death. As a gesture, they gave us the funeral cars for free, which I thought was lovely of them. When Marie rang them to see if Garry had arrived and that he was being taken care of, Harry reassured her. 'We are looking after him for you, don't have any worries,' he told her.

Our local vicar, Canon Stephen Attwater, from Christ Church in Padgate, came to see me and was very kind and thoughtful. He'd heard about Garry's death while on holiday and couldn't believe it had happened so close to his church. I'd met him once at a christening and thought he was a nice man, so we decided to hold the funeral there. He visited the family a few times to discuss the funeral. He asked about Garry and what he liked and disliked. What was his personality and beliefs? Strangely, talking to a man of the cloth seemed to be cathartic. I was questioning God myself after what had happened, but I knew that I had to make Garry's passage a calm and soulful one. However, the girls struggled with their faith and they had every right to question their beliefs. My brother-in-law Mark, Marie's husband, is so kind and gentle and a larger-than-life person, but he is not an openly emotional man. However, after the vicar left, Mark went for a walk in the grounds of the church to try to find solace and peace over what had happened to Garry and how the family were suffering. It was his way of coping and I understood. We all deal with grief differently, and we need to understand that and treat each other with respect. Our bodies and minds have clever mechanisms to help us recover gently and slowly – and hopefully get back to a degree of normality, whatever we perceive that to be.

The aspect of the funeral in which the girls and I had the most involvement was the songs. Garry's love of music was all-encompassing and it was important that we got this element of the service just right. One evening, the four of us sat down and talked through what he might like. Elton John was one of his all-time favourites, so it was easy to choose 'Goodbye Yellow Brick Road' and 'Candle In The Wind'. He loved disco too, so 'Night Fever' by the Bee Gees was another good one. We were 'umming' and 'aahing' over various other choices when Zoe stopped us mid-flow.

'I know!' she said. 'He loved that song – what was it? – "Living In a Box"!'

Well, almost the second the words came out of her mouth she looked dumbstruck. Talk about laugh, we had to dry our eyes!

'Oh, Zoe,' I said when we'd all calmed down, 'I don't think that's appropriate. Imagine what Nana and Granddad would say!' That just set us off again.

Daft as it sounds, that bit of black humour did us all a lot of good. It was the first time we'd laughed in weeks and it released a lot of the tension. Garry would've seen the humour in it, that's for sure, and he would have laughed the longest and loudest. It would have tickled his sense of humour all right.

Monday, 3 September was the date set for the funeral, just over three weeks after Garry's death. It was going to be the first time I'd left the house since coming back from the hospital, and as the date crept closer I felt more and more distressed about it. I thought I would collapse in a heap the moment I stepped out of my front door, and nothing could quell the rising tide of panic I felt when I thought about the ordeal ahead.

That said, like a true Northern woman I was determined to have my hair done for the funeral. I wanted to look my best for my husband, which might sound a bit strange to some people, but I'm sure most married women can relate to that. The hairdresser's that we always went to booked me in, and Marie and I drove over there. The staff did not know what to say as they were as devastated as everyone else. They could hardly believe that they would not see Garry come in with his three daughters and joke around with them. He loved his hair to look trendy and 'with it' as he laughed with the girls. However, he would faint when he had to pay the bill. He said that he knew they would spend every penny of his money, but the joy would be when he got older they would all look after him. I put on my bravest face as we tried to keep the conversation to the trivial stuff you talk about at the hairdresser's, but it was stiff and difficult.

Driving back and forth down our road was a struggle. I insisted that we drove around the spot where Garry lay as I felt physically sick going over the spot. It seemed so disrespectful.

Back home, I just sat in the lounge and stared out of the window. Suddenly, something caught my eye: a flash of shiny yellow somewhere inside the subway. There were a couple of guys in there, wearing high-visibility vests and carrying large poles with brushes on the end. Close to the entrance of the subway, another guy was picking litter out of the bushes. A Warrington Borough Council van was parked nearby. I shouted to Marie, who was staying with us that weekend, and she stood at my side as we watched the workmen make the subway and its surroundings all spick and span.

'I can't bloody believe it,' I said. 'All these months we've been asking them to tidy that place up. Now they know the telly's coming, they've got their bloody fingers out!'

I was livid. If it takes a high-profile murder case to get a filthy subway made litter- and graffiti-free, that's a very sad indictment of our society.

They had put two litter bins either side of the subway soon after Garry's death, which the officer in charge of the case himself noticed when he was showing the Chief Constable of Cheshire the scene, and now, after months of ignoring the local community's pleas, they were cleaning the subway!

'I feel like going out and giving them both barrels,' I said. 'It's just sick.'

'It's not their fault,' said Marie, clutching my arm. 'It's not right, I agree, but they're only doing their jobs. You've been good so far. Let's get through the funeral, and see what happens after that.'

She was right, of course, but it didn't make me feel any better. They were doing all this just because Sky TV were coming, the hypocrites. My emotions were all over the place, I wasn't sleeping and anger was always bubbling close to the iron control I held on myself, so it took very little to get me going.

The night before the funeral was another sleepless one. I lay in bed, eyes wide open, trying to imagine how I would cope with standing by Garry's coffin in just a few hours' time. Amy was still sleeping in my bed, and I lay still because I wanted her to get as much sleep as she could. I fretted about the girls – would they cope, and how would they manage if I fell to pieces in front of them? I thought of all the cameras on us, waiting for the moment we broke down, and all those pairs of eyes silently watching as we passed by.

The thought made me feel physically sick, and the feeling only increased as I dragged myself out of bed when dawn broke. I tried to put on my bravest face and disguise the bags of tiredness from under my eyes. The girls woke up – if they'd managed to sleep, which is doubtful – and queued for the bathroom. There was none of the usual teenage bickering and banter; the house was deeply subdued that morning as we waited for the cars to arrive.

At 12.30 p.m., the first of the shiny, black limousines pulled up outside the house. My knees began to wobble and I felt nauseous. I steadied myself, knowing there would be press everywhere. The girls braced themselves too, and I gave them all a hug. God, they were so brave that day. Distraught as they were, there was no question they wouldn't attend their dad's funeral. I knew I needed to find the courage they were showing. 'Do it for Garry,' I said to myself over and over. But as our front door opened I lost my nerve.

'I can't do it,' I said to Marie and Keith, who were holding on to my arm. 'I just can't do it. I'm not going.'

'You can do it,' Marie said from behind me. 'Look, the girls have already gone ahead. They're waiting for you.'

With great dignity, Zoe, Danielle and Amy had walked down our drive and into the limousine. I could see them looking at me expectantly, but I was rooted to the spot. If it hadn't been for Keith, who took my elbow and gently steered me down the path, I'm not sure I could've gone any further. I was like a robot putting one foot in front of the other. I climbed into the car and just broke down. Perhaps that helped, because by the time we reached the church I was composed enough to be at my rightful place next to my daughters, who needed my love and support so much now.

What we couldn't believe was the amount of press covering the funeral. They had climbed up trees and were standing on walls to get a better view. We could've done without it, of course, but I understood that they had a job to do. It was also at that moment that it began to dawn on me what an impact Garry's murder had had across the country. I'd read some of the letters and talked to friends, but I wasn't prepared for this level of interest in the case. That was echoed too in the number of people inside the church. The press said there were about 200 there; it certainly looked packed, and there were also people standing outside.

Through my tears, I recognised friends and work colleagues of Garry's, plus many people I knew. I was particularly pleased to see my old boss, an observant Jew who perhaps wouldn't have come to a Christian service. But there he was, paying his respects, and I was very moved to see him. The police officers who had been so kind and helpful over the previous three horrendous weeks were also there, as were local people I didn't know, but who had come to show their solidarity with us.

It was the longest 40 minutes of my life. Garry's brother and nephews carried the coffin into the church. It was covered with a huge bouquet of roses that I'd picked. We sang 'Amazing Grace' – one of Garry's favourites that he always enjoyed playing on his keyboard. Then Canon Attwater got up to speak. He didn't know Garry but nevertheless he paid a fitting tribute to him.

'When Garry died three weeks ago, the light went out for Helen and Zoe, Danielle and Amy,' he said. 'Garry was central to their lives. He was a loving, caring, devoted family man and there is no doubt he will be sadly missed. He enjoyed meeting people. He was very much the life and soul of the party. He had a great sense of humour and, when cancer came, he fought it off with characteristic bravery. And so there is a tremendous amount to thank God for when we reflect upon Garry's life.'

After that, a soloist sang 'Ave Maria'. It was beautiful and haunting, as it had also been sung at our wedding 21 years earlier. I'm glad the *Sky News* camera – the only one we'd allowed in, to supply images for everyone else – wasn't on my face at that moment. Marie was due to read the well-known poem 'Footprints', but when the moment came she couldn't do it, knowing she'd break down. So Canon Attwater stepped in and read it.

Following the Final Commendation, it was time to leave, but there was one more thing I wanted to do. My legs wobbling, I made my way out of the bench and asked Harry, the funeral director, if I could kiss Garry's coffin. Of course I could, he said, and with the heaviest of hearts I made the simple gesture of farewell to my beloved husband before stepping outside the church and into the late-summer sunshine and the glare of the flashbulbs.

The final stop on this most awful of journeys was the crematorium at Walton Lea. This was to be a private event, just for family and a few friends. The police gave us an escort up there and, as far as I knew, the press respected our request and didn't follow us. In contrast to the church, the crematorium was cold and impersonal – one in, one out – but I suppose that is how they work. A few words were said, the coffin disappeared behind the curtain and that was that. Dazed, we wandered outside and looked at all the flowers people had sent, along with their messages of sympathy. I stared at them, barely able to take in the sentiment and emotion with which they were written. Then we made our way to the local church hall for a wake in memory of Garry, which my parents had been good enough to pay for.

Once the wake was over, we returned home, wrung out and exhausted by the day's events. The girls watched some of the coverage on TV but I couldn't face it. I went to bed and managed to sleep reasonably well, relieved that one of the worst days of my life was over. Of course, I knew it was not the end of the ordeal, by any stretch of the imagination, and I would have to find the strength to carry on and be strong for the family when the court case began. The wheel was just going round and round. Where do we stop next?

TEN

A New Reality

The day after Garry's funeral started with something of a setback. There was coverage of the funeral in all the papers, as we expected, but one tabloid had decided to print some of the private messages attached to the flowers we'd left behind at the crematorium. I was hurt and annoyed, because we'd cooperated with the press and allowed them to cover the funeral itself if they left us in peace at the crematorium. Obviously, that agreement had been flouted and they must have sneaked in when we'd gone. I felt it was a betrayal of our trust, but there wasn't a lot I could do and, besides, the majority of the press had complied with our request and in general had treated us with respect and courtesy. I decided to let it go. In any case, there were more urgent matters to deal with.

The days passed. 'What now?' I asked myself. I had to adjust to a new reality – that of widow and single parent. Garry's input into family life was gone; all the things he might have dealt with were now my responsibility. One of the first issues was getting around. At some point before they attacked Garry, the yobs had damaged my car, a Renault Scenic, which the police had taken away to examine for forensic evidence. When it was returned, it was covered in deep dents down the side. I looked at it and shuddered. If they could make such an impact on metal with their feet, what the hell had they done to Garry's skull? I couldn't keep something that so cruelly represented the circumstances of Garry's death. It had to go, and my brother-in-law helped me to find another one. Even today, when I see a Renault Scenic my blood runs cold and I have to look away.

There was also all the financial stuff to sort out – the kind of task that's hard to face at the best of times, never mind the worst. Thank God I had Keith and Mark to help me wade through bank accounts, insurance policies, mortgage agreements, pensions and salary arrangements. The girls' phones were all on contract under Garry's name, so they had to go through the usual 'press one . . . press two . . . press three' hassle to get them changed. Keith and Mark were brilliant; they took Garry's laptop and went through it methodically, figuring out where all the virtual paperwork was kept. Garry's employers were very respectful and assisted us in getting all Garry's IT and phones over to them as smoothly and as painlessly as possible. When I went to watch the film *PS I Love You* on the big screen, having read the book beforehand, I was struck by the scene where the character Holly has lost her husband and rings his phone to hear his voice on his voicemail message. If only I had kept Garry's phone, I could have done that. Small things come into your head and make you think, 'What if I had done that?'

I couldn't think about going back to work then, and my company were very good about it. They told me they would keep me on full pay for six months while I decided what to do. They knew I would have the court case to face, which obviously would delay that decision, but they never once pressured me into anything. People may not realise how their small acts of kindness can have such a huge effect on the people they help. For me, this financial buffer stilled my panic. Overnight, I became the main wage earner responsible for three daughters.

I had to summon all my strength to fight for justice for Garry through the courts, and worrying about keeping a roof over our heads at the same time would have sapped me further. I am so grateful to them.

Garry's death also had a huge impact on family members, both practically and emotionally. Keith, Marie and Mark had been wonderful, but, once they had dealt with all the paperwork and waded through other tasks, I felt I couldn't ask them to do any more. My instinct was to cling on to them but that wasn't fair. They had lives to get on with, and Keith was spending a lot of time and money flying back and forth from Spain. Marie was cooking our meals, shopping and doing other domestic jobs in the house. They both needed an emotional and physical breather from us. They needed to be with their loved ones and try to get back to some sort of normality.

Naturally, my mum and dad were devastated by what had happened, but it was a few weeks after Garry's death before I could see my dad. He was (and still is) in a care home and I hadn't wanted to see him because I thought the shock of him facing me, in my grief, would be too much for him. I was so frightened of him having a heart attack because his health was so very frail. Also, I didn't want the press to follow me and find out where he was. I knew from Marie that he was deeply worried about me but I couldn't bring myself to inflict my pain and suffering on him. When we finally met, he just broke down, as I thought he would.

'What kind of dad am I,' he sobbed, 'stuck in a care home and unable to protect his daughter?' He ranted and raved. 'What kind of world are we living in today?' he shouted. 'Garry didn't deserve this to happen to him.'

As much as I tried to console and reassure him, he was devastated. Dad just wanted to be able to come out of the home and protect us. When a man cries, it is very hard to watch, and even more so when it is your dad. My dad is a very proud working-class man, the head of the family, there to support and care for everyone. Now he was so angry both at losing Garry like we did and at the fact that he was unable to be there for us.

My mum's health has also deteriorated because of the whole experience, and her heart has become very fragile.

When something like this happens, it's like a stone being dropped into a pond: the ripples spread out far and wide. People who commit crime – and not just serious crime – never seem to understand the effects of their criminality, not just on the immediate victim but on so many other people too. Criminals seem unwilling or unable to take any kind of responsibility for their actions – if they did, and they actually thought before they acted, they might not act at all. It seems to be complete thoughtlessness and lack of respect and responsibility that is to blame for so much crime across the world. It is very sad, and its consequences are devastating for individuals and communities alike.

I believe that lack of communication and empathy, the inability to put oneself in a victim's place, is the cause for so much violent crime. If we can get at minor offenders early enough and make them see the end product of their actions, understand the on-going suffering they are inflicting on so many, not just the immediate victim, for years to come, perhaps we can prevent atrocities like personal attacks. I speak to many young people in my work today, and this is the message I try to get them to remember and to influence their friends, deflecting them from violence. It isn't easy sharing our personal story with strangers, especially as I am a very private person, but it helps me make some sense of Garry's life.

Now it was just the four of us, and we were still all finding it hard to sleep, Amy in particular; she was still only twelve and not much more than a baby. I was tempted to go back on the sleeping tablets but I didn't want to be dependent and robotic. I had to keep focused for the girls, though it wasn't easy. One of my biggest worries was how we were going to cope in this house, packed as it was with so many memories of Garry. Actually, it wasn't so much the house but the street. People constantly asked me if and when we were going to move, and at first I dug my heels in, not wanting to leave Garry's aura behind. Then, when I started going out in the car, I realised that something had to give. I had to pass the spot where Garry lay on the ground and I still always swerved to avoid it, but seeing other cars drive over the top of it made me cringe. Besides, Amy was suffering terrible flashbacks, having moved back into her room at the front of the house, and her lack of sleep was turning her into a zombie. If we had any chance of learning to live in the new reality imposed on us, I realised we had to leave our family home.

I decided to rent a house a few miles away from everything to try and give the girls some solace. It's pleasantly leafy, quite posh, I suppose, and I thought it would be somewhere nice for the girls to be for a while. I would give it six months and see how we got on. I let my immediate neighbours know, as they would have wondered what was going on and worried. I also asked them not to tell anyone where we'd gone, as I didn't want the press to know. If and when a trial began, the last thing I wanted was photographers camped outside our door. The neighbours understood, and were sorry to see us go. I think a few of the men living close by felt guilty about the trouble that had befallen us. Maybe they thought that if they'd come to Garry's rescue, or had stood shoulder-to-shoulder with him, none of it would've happened. I know that, if it had happened to someone else down the road, Garry would've felt just the same. Perhaps they were right, but hindsight is a wonderful thing and life doesn't always work out so neatly. We parted as friends and as neighbours who had tried to do something to protect our community, for which Garry had paid the ultimate price.

I believe our neighbours typified what we mean when we talk about good communities; they were the bedrock of ours. Many of us live on big estates and never see anyone from day to day. In fact, that has happened to us. No one says 'hello' – they're too busy going to work and doing school runs. That is why I loved living in Fearnhead, with fantastic neighbours whom I classed as friends. I don't know if it is because I had been brought up with going in and out of our next-door neighbours' houses, but I felt that this was what we could do living there. We respected their space but knew we would help one another and could enjoy chatting over the garden fence. Garry would wash the cars religiously on Sunday mornings and so did Eric across the road, both of them chatting and talking about cars. That was their passion. The decision to move away was not an easy one.

Still, I wasn't getting rid of the old house. I didn't put it on the market or rent it out. I couldn't bring myself to do it; it was Garry's last home and the thought of someone else in there, so soon after his death, gave me the shivers. The family helped us pack, which was very difficult indeed. I didn't touch his stuff and took only what we needed. I didn't want to think the move was permanent – which, inevitably, it was. Our house was a spacious, attractive home, set in a warm community, which, ironically, had been made safer because of what had happened. It was full of such happy family memories and laughter that I like to think have sunk into the bricks and fabric of the house. I hope other people will make it their own happy home, fill it up with their experiences and memories. But, for me, as I turned the key that day, it was the last time. There could be no going back.

* * *

Moving house is always an upheaval, but mostly it's all positive and a change for the good. I had very mixed feelings about leaving Garry's last home, and, nice as our new environment was, one of us was missing. The move didn't feel like a family decision, just one made out of necessity. But with hindsight I'm glad we did it. We left in October 2007, and the following month the trial of Swellings, Sorton and Cunliffe, plus two others, was due to start. I'm very glad I wasn't still living there on the day the judge and jury visited to inspect the spot where Garry was attacked.

The forthcoming trial was unsettling us all. The girls knew they would have to give evidence in court and this was causing them no end of stress, not least Amy. Although we'd moved her, the flashbacks and nightmares stubbornly refused to go away, and she was terrified of going to sleep. From the day that Garry died, she had come into our bed and my poor little 12 year old reverted to being a younger child. I would hold her to get her to sleep. I took her to the doctor and told him that, while I didn't condone giving sleeping tablets to children, Amy's case was exceptional and there must be something healthy and non-addictive he could find to get her through this.

'She's completely out of her sleep cycle,' I said, 'and I think she needs to have something to restore it.'

I could tell by the doctor's face that he understood because of our circumstances but he wasn't happy. 'I don't think it's appropriate at her age,' he said, 'despite what she's going through. Don't you think it would be better if she sees a therapist?'

'I don't want a therapist,' Amy said. 'I don't want to talk to anyone. I just want to sleep properly!'

He could see how distressed she was, and that I was almost begging him to make an exception, but he wouldn't budge. I was disgusted. I had spoken to Marie, who was a nursing sister, and she felt that, in Amy's case, her lack of sleep had become so bad that she needed something strong from the doctor to enable her to get back into some kind of a normal sleeping pattern. It wasn't my intention to keep her on sleeping tablets forever, just to give her some temporary relief from her pain and suffering.

I will try to explain how this terrible experience felt to us as a family. When we go to the movies, we like being scared by werewolves, vampires and axe murderers. We like the blood and gore, the creeping up behind you, the shock and horror, but we know we are safe, that it can't hurt us. On that hot summer's night, my young daughters came face to face with evil that surpasses anything that a creative film director or talented scriptwriter can ever invent. They saw the blood and gore. They saw the painful death of their father. This was reality, not something you can leave behind with the popcorn and soft drinks. This was not a violent video game that you can pause and rewind or restart the level and bring the hero back to life. I only wish I could.

Amy was adamant that she didn't want to see a therapist, so we tried as many herbal supplements as we could. However, nothing worked and the sleepless situation went on for ages, until, a few months down the line, her night-time patterns started to settle down normally again.

Needless to say, the girls weren't back at school yet, and were nowhere near ready to go. It was Danielle's GCSE year, but she couldn't face the stares and whispers of her classmates. The school was very good and said they would be guided by me as their parent, which I thought was a very sensible approach. Even home schooling was out of the question in the first few months after their dad's death; they simply couldn't take anything in. I now realise that they were all suffering from extreme post-traumatic stress.

They weren't alone. Increasingly, I was plagued by terrible thoughts and there were days when I just couldn't get out of bed. The girls would become very upset and panicky when they saw me like this and, although I tried to be strong most of the time, there were occasions when I felt I hadn't another ounce of fight left in me. Marie saw what was happening to me and told me I needed to get up, get dressed and get through the day – for the sake of the girls, if nothing else. My mum was out of her mind with worry at what the shock might do to me.

I'll be honest. There were days when I wondered what the point of living was. Now I can see that Marie and the girls were picking up on this, but then, in my own bubble of misery and despair, it was sometimes hard to see beyond what I was feeling. I couldn't – and wouldn't – have done anything to myself. The girls had already lost their dad; imagine if they lost their mum too? But the dark thoughts were there, particularly on the opening day of the trial at Chester Crown Court.

ELEVEN

Justice for Garry

I was determined from the start to attend every day of the trial. Desperate as I felt, I wouldn't be intimidated by the five in the dock or their families. I wanted to go in with my head held high to show them that they would never get to me. As I had worked as a legal secretary, I was quite comfortable around courtrooms, and, as a family, we'd been to Chester Crown Court before the trial started so we could familiarise ourselves with it. It's an old building, a bit draughty and echoey like a lot of older courtrooms up and down the country. They don't serve the needs of modern justice very well, I have to say, but at the present time we're stuck with them.

On the first day of the trial, Wednesday, 14 November 2007, I walked into court and took my seat, hoping and praying we would get justice. As the five defendants arrived in the dock, I immediately felt sick and light-headed. It was the first time I'd clapped eyes on them, and the pain that surged through me at that moment was as raw and as searing as it had ever been. I clutched the rail in front of me for support, then clung on to Marie, sitting by my side. All five were of slight build and to me looked not much more than children. They seemed subdued and sat there, just staring into the distance. Few observers could have thought them capable of the terrible crime they were charged with.

We sat in the courtroom along with the one prosecuting QC and his team, while we watched each row being filled up with an army of defence teams. There must have been at least 15 people. Each defendant had a QC and there were also junior barristers, along with solicitors and their staff.

Over the next few weeks, the defendants' innocent facade started to crack and their true natures, as well as their attitude to the whole court system, became obvious to everyone.

'Oh my God, look at them,' I whispered to Marie one day. 'They're laughing at us. They're laughing at the whole thing.'

They began shuffling, sniggering, grinning at relatives and looking generally relaxed and carefree. In the dock, the five of them could have been on a school trip. I had to turn my head away in disgust and try to concentrate on the legal arguments as the trial and the days rolled on.

However, on that first day it just seemed to be an awful lot of 'housekeeping'. Because some of the boys were juveniles, a request known as 'special measures' was put before the judge, Mr Justice Andrew Smith, regarding the wearing of his formal robes, which could be seen as intimidating to a young person in the dock.

Back home after that first day, I walked into the kitchen, a large, open-plan space with a sofa at one end. I sat down, trying to put the defendants' faces out of my mind. At the side of the sofa there was a table, with a pot containing Garry's ashes. I hadn't decided what to do with them but for the moment I wanted them near me. They were somehow comforting.

'Oh, Garry,' I said, 'what's happening? I feel I've let you down. Today was a circus. I wish you were here.'

There was no response. Give or take the occasional creak of the house settling down for the night, it was silent. I looked at

Garry's ashes, then over to the cupboard where I kept various bottles of sleeping tablets, painkillers and the like. I got up and opened the cupboard. There were enough pills in there to ease my pain forever. A half-empty bottle of wine stood nearby.

'What is the point of going on? What is it all about?'

I went and sat down again. The people who would find me the following morning would be the ones I'd least want to hurt in the world. Could I really do that to my children, and in the middle of all this? I wouldn't condemn anyone who made this terrible choice, and chose death. At that moment, such a release was all I wanted. But I just couldn't do it to them. I lay down on the sofa and began to cry; a flood of tears for Garry wrapped up in guilty ones for the thoughts I was having.

The next morning when the police arrived at 7 a.m. to help me prepare for court that day, I wasn't even dressed.

'You're best off staying at home,' the family liaison police officer said when she saw me. 'Going to court today won't do you any good. Try to sleep. The rest of the family will go instead and we will promise to let you know what happened.'

On the following Monday, Michael Chambers QC opened the prosecution case. He described how Station Road North had been plagued by gangs causing trouble, and how when Garry went out to remonstrate with a group of youths, including the five in the dock, he was attacked.

'He had had the courage to go out and face them,' he said, 'but they were in no mood to be challenged. He was no match for their combined assault. One of them kicked him so hard that his training shoe came off and was found lodged under Mr Newlove's body.'

I swallowed hard, trying not to think of the owner of that shoe kicking Garry like a dog. I thought of the terrible dents on my car, which proved the violence and sheer brutal force behind each kick. Then I thought of Garry's defenceless head and body and I felt like vomiting. Mr Chambers was not using emotive language – he was trying to outline the facts of the case as plainly as possible – but every word twisted into me like a knife. He told the jury that all five were charged with murder in a 'joint enterprise', that is, that they'd all played a part in Garry's death, whether by threatening, punching, kicking, supporting or egging one another on. He added, 'The prosecution are confident that these five are responsible for this fatal assault, although others may be involved as well.'

My only wish was that everyone who had been there that night was in the dock, facing the same charge. Garry had 14 kicks to the head and sustained 40 internal injuries to his body in a matter of a few minutes. There were more than 15 youths around him at one stage. I was pleased even this eminent prosecutor could see, like we all could, that this was a mob attack.

At the end of the day's proceedings, I went home, shocked and stunned by what I'd seen and heard. I was truly grateful that although the girls had come with me, as witnesses they were placed in a separate part of the building so they could not hear the brutal facts. I was careful not to discuss anything with the girls, as they were the prosecution's key witnesses and would be making their appearances in court later. We tried to chat about other things but we were having conversations that were going nowhere. It was very hard indeed to ignore the elephant in the room. Eventually, the girls trooped off to bed, leaving me alone with my tormented thoughts. I thought about Garry, and how he was referred to in court as 'Man A', as the prosecution outlined exactly how the others (named B, C, D, E and F) had surrounded him. Man A . . . no longer Garry Newlove, husband and father, but a letter of the alphabet, a mere statistic.

Exhausted, I stayed at home the following day. Besides, it

was the day the jury would be visiting Station Road North and there was no way I wanted to be caught up in that. Once they had made the visit, the case would recommence on Monday, 19 November. After one of the darkest moments I'd ever had in my life, I was determined to pull myself together and see the case through to the end. There was no way that rabble in the dock would stop me from seeing justice done. I would certainly be there on that Monday because the girls would be giving their evidence and they needed 100 per cent of my support.

As juveniles, Amy and Danielle could give their evidence by video link from another room in the building, but as Zoe was 18 she would have to appear in person. She could apply for a screen to be placed around the witness box, which I thought was a good idea. However, Zoe was adamant that she didn't want this and so we had something of a wrangle about it. I admired her courage, but I felt instinctively that she needed to be protected. Swellings was older than her, and a big lad. I didn't want him or any of the others putting her off, so I put my foot down and insisted the screens went up. The defence weren't keen and they objected, but they were overruled. It's a good job they were too, because if those defendants could have got into the witness box they would have. It was an absolute joke. Zoe was already in the box with the screens around it when the five were brought up into the dock and they were stretching up as far as possible to try to see over the top of the screen. I was mortified and felt like screaming, 'How sick are you?' Garry's nephews, Jarrod and Glynn, were sitting across the room so that Zoe could look at them for reassurance and support, but they were on the receiving end of 'hard-man' stares from the dock and in the end one of them stopped coming to the trial because of the silent threat. It was so confrontational and he didn't want to be goaded into disrespecting Garry's memory in any way – emotions were close to boiling over. It was outrageous; a volatile situation that made life very uncomfortable indeed for us, the victims.

Each defendant had a QC representing him; top lawyers, highly skilled with words, whose job was to cast doubt on the safety of the evidence being placed in front of the jury. No wonder Zoe was shaking in the witness box that day. Thankfully, Mr Justice Smith was a very fair and honourable man and he made sure the defence team didn't go too far. Mind you, Zoe stood no nonsense. At one point, one of the defending QCs made a comment about Garry 'bullying' the defendants prior to the attack. Immediately, Zoe shot back. 'Do you mean like the way you're questioning me now?' she said. Then she spoke the words that would be quoted in most of the following day's newspapers and on TV, words that still chill me to the bone even today:

'The lads started to kick him,' she said. 'They were kicking him like they would kick a football. They were laughing at him and then they started to run off.'

I breathed hard, trying desperately not to break down. It was the first time I'd heard any of this. It might seem strange, but as a family we'd never discussed exactly what the girls had seen that night. They didn't volunteer any information and I didn't ask them about it. Even today, there are probably bits and pieces I don't know. I didn't want to put them through it and I think they were too scared of the effect it might have on me to tell me the whole truth. I often think that when they are fully grown women and when time has passed, we may be strong enough to put all the pieces of the jigsaw together, but that's for the future.

Zoe went on to describe how she grabbed Cunliffe's shirt and wouldn't let go, even though he was chopping at her hand to get free. One of them also punched Tom, Zoe's boyfriend, and she was terrified they would set about him the way they'd just laid into Garry. She spoke clearly, almost angrily. There was no doubt that her evidence was very compelling. She'd never been in a courtroom in her life but she's a bright girl and she knew that, above everything else, she was speaking up in her dad's memory. When she'd finished, the defendants were taken back down again and she was allowed to leave the courtroom. I went outside with her and gave her a big hug. She wanted to sit in on the rest of the day's proceedings, which she was entitled to do, but I didn't think it was a great idea, so my nephew took her home.

It was now Danielle and Amy's turn to give evidence. Danielle's was dealt with relatively quickly. In a taped police interview played in court, she told how she'd put Garry in the recovery position as he lay on the pavement, saying, 'I saw he was halfway dead. He was on his side. I checked him and there was a lot of blood. All around his head was covered in blood.'

By the time Danielle had finished, it was 4.30 p.m. The judge said he was concerned that it was a bit late in the day for Amy to begin her evidence and would be steered by me, as her parent, whether to carry on or adjourn until the following day. I had a quick word with the police, who were worried that if we adjourned I might be accused of 'coaching' Amy overnight.

'I don't care what they say,' I said. 'Amy's been here since nine this morning and she's been through hell. We're going home together.'

The judge seemed happy with that and so off we went.

We took Amy back the following morning and she finally appeared on video link. What I hadn't realised up to this point was that, although Amy was talking directly to the barristers and the judge, there were TV screens in court and everyone could see her quite clearly, including the defendants. So, really, the video link was pointless. She might as well have just stood there in open court, for all the protection she was getting. I was angry, but I didn't want to show it because Amy had been told to show as little emotion as possible, not to fidget or look awkward in any way. Very hard for a 13-year-old girl at the best of times, but almost impossible under these circumstances. But she did it; she was very good and very clear, even under intensive cross-examination. Before she gave her evidence live, a taped police interview, filmed a few days after Garry's death, was played. She described how she had been in her room when she heard a bang outside and the sound of laughing. She followed her dad outside as he confronted them.

'They punched and shoved him,' she said. 'One went behind him and kneed him in the back and he fell. I could hear the sound of the blows. They were kicking his head – three or four of them were hitting his head.

'I ran up to them. They crowded round him. Some walked away but one turned back for more and one was still hitting him. I pushed one of them as he kicked him.

'I closed my eyes and don't remember who I hit. I just kept hitting. I got angry and I just closed my eyes. I saw Dad on the floor, bleeding on the side of his head. He had cuts and grazes on his face. I was crying. I didn't know what I was doing. I didn't want to look at him.'

Remember, Amy was only 12 years old when this happened to her, and had just turned 13 before the trial began. One day, Swellings, Sorton and Cunliffe will be released from prison. They will be reunited with their families and maybe resume normal lives. Amy's trauma, and that of Zoe, Danielle and myself, will ease in time, but it will never go away. Swellings, Sorton and Cunliffe might put it all behind them, but in my eyes they are scum and always will be.

Our neighbour (I'll call her A to protect her identity), who witnessed the attack, gave evidence next. She'd seen what had happened and come rushing out to help in the immediate chaos and aftermath of the attack. She knew some of the defendants' families, so she was brave to come up to the witness stand. The defence tried to tie her up in knots over a description of one of the defendants that had become confused, but she stuck to her guns and told the jury that the gang had dived on Garry like 'a pack of animals'.

Then it was my turn. I was told that, instead of my taking the stand, my evidence could be read out and it would stand or fall on its merits. As I hadn't actually seen the attack, I couldn't add anything to the descriptions of the accused. My contribution was to describe the noises I'd heard, which Garry had gone out to investigate, and to relate the story of what happened when I discovered him dying in the road. I told the jury that I'd seen a trainer print in the centre of his forehead, a kind of 'V-shape in blood' as I think I put it at the time, but I hadn't been sure whether it was made by a heel or a toe.

This piece of evidence, which I provided on oath, was discounted because no bruising could be found on Garry's forehead that might relate to it. I swear that I saw it, though, and so did my mum.

After an adjournment, the forensic evidence was presented. This was a part of the trial I just couldn't sit through. I didn't want to know how my husband had been cut up during an autopsy in a mortuary, and what had been discovered. What I know is that he was kicked fourteen times, receiving forty internal injuries, and one of those kicks killed him. To me, it doesn't matter who delivered the fatal kick, although that was argued over at the time. The fact was they were *all* there and those convicted were as guilty as one another. No one attempted to stop the violence, and they all knew what kind of violence they were capable of. That is the law of joint enterprise and, while there are those who challenge it, I say it is a good one and should remain in the law books. If some of those involved were standing there watching, why didn't they get help? I heard them all laughing as they attacked Garry. My daughters saw it happen.

Anyway, it would've done me no good to hear the pathologist's report, especially when Marie sat through it and later told me it made for 'horrendous' listening. She's been a nurse for many years and she knows what she's talking about. A few months ago, I looked at Garry's death certificate and decided to Google some of the medical terms. I only got so far when I had to stop. It wasn't worth it, not for the sake of my sanity.

In December, it was the defendants' turn to give evidence. I was keen to hear this, though I was sickened when Swellings laughed as his barrister described him as a 'black sheep'. Some of the language the boys used was way beyond what kids of their age and background might come out with – it was clear to me that there'd been some 'coaching' along the way. They were coming out with specific phrases you'd only use if you had a legal background and I was dying to stand up and say, 'Can you explain exactly what that means?'

We heard that it was very likely that some of the defendants had been involved in attacks on two other people just before Garry was attacked. We also had to sit through long periods of evidence during which the defendants blamed one another, like the cowards they are. Sorton apparently confessed to his mother while in custody that he'd punched Garry in the face and that he 'hadn't meant to do it'. He also said he'd tripped over Garry's body on the way to tell a police officer and he'd lost his shoe. Having previously heard that Garry had been kicked with such force that a training shoe had been lodged under his body, it wasn't hard to realise what a whole load of bull he was coming out with. Swellings even tried to blame Garry for what had happened, saying Garry was 'angry' when he confronted them about the damage they were causing to the cars and the digger.

So that made it OK to kill him? I didn't know whether to laugh or cry. The whole thing was ludicrous.

The trial then took a break for Christmas – the first for the Newlove family without Garry. Naturally, I didn't want any kind of celebration but the girls had been through so much and I felt I had to do something for their sakes. I bought them a few presents, put up a tree and made Christmas dinner. The girls tried to enjoy it as best they could, but, to be honest, we were all robots that day, just going through the motions. I didn't want anyone around to join us, and I didn't accept any invites to other people's homes. I wanted us to be together so that we could find the collective strength to get through the day and the rest of the time until the trial started again. New Year's Eve was equally difficult but we battled through, and by the time January came we were ready once more to face the ordeal of the trial.

On 2 January 2008, Mr Justice Smith began his summing up. He told the jury it was the prosecution case that all five defendants jointly murdered Garry, and he also defined what 'murder' actually means in law.

The following day, the jury went out to consider their verdict, and so began the longest wait of my life. Of course, I don't know what they were talking about in there but to me it was an open-and-shut case. The police seemed to be getting worried about the length of time it was taking. Finally, we were brought back into court on 16 January. The jury had reached a verdict: guilty of murder in the cases of Adam Swellings, Stephen Sorton and Jordan Cunliffe, and not guilty in the cases of the two other juveniles on trial.

I burst into tears when the verdicts were announced, and so did the girls, who were at home that day and found out via a newsflash on the TV. It was a mixture of relief that three had been convicted, and anger and frustration that two hadn't.

Sorton's mum was also crying. I could see she was distraught. It turned out that she'd made him go to the police when he initially admitted being at the scene of the attack. Maybe she thought he'd be treated leniently. Swellings' parents were devastated too. But I had no sympathy for any of them. I brought my kids up to be respectful of others, not to go round in a gang, drunk out of their minds and intimidating or attacking anyone in their path. If you're a parent and you have no idea where your child is at night or what they are doing, you have to accept responsibility for what might happen to them. That's what being a parent is about.

I felt as if I would have a heart attack with all the emotions that were swirling around the courtroom that day. But I had to keep calm, as there was one thing I was determined to do, and that I'd been planning for a while. There was to be a Cheshire Police press conference at Chester Racecourse the following day, during which I would read a statement about the impact Garry's murder — for that's now what it officially was — had on me and my family. The police had previously asked me if, on a guilty verdict, I would 'say a few words', and, if I agreed, they would help me to put something together with the aid of some set questions. I knew this would be my only chance to speak for Garry the person, and I readily agreed to do it. I started typing and, over the course of a few evenings at home, managed to put something together. I wrote and rewrote it before finally sending it off to the police press office for consideration.

'Is it all right?' I asked the press officer nervously.

'It's more than all right, Helen,' she replied. 'It's amazing. We never expected you to write this.

I wasn't going to let Garry down now. I would have my say, for me, for the girls, but most of all for Garry. Then we would fade into the background and rebuild our lives away from public sight. That was the plan, but it didn't quite work out that way!

So, in front of a packed room of reporters, photographers and camera people, I started to read the statement. I have reproduced it in full below, as it sums up everything I felt about Garry, before and after his death.

Garry was a caring, loving, funny and most of all a family man. We did everything together for 26 years. He adored his daughters, always attended their school sports days and parents' evenings. Always keen to encourage them to achieve their best. Garry loved cars and music. Every Sunday he would wash his car religiously. We did everything together: shopping, hairdresser's, you name it, we did it as a family unit. Garry loved doing jobs around the house with Amy. When they did the gardening, he would call her his own 'Charlie Dimmock'. They were like a double act.

The light has gone out of our lives. It's like a piece of our jigsaw has been lost for ever. The tiniest of things that we used to do as a family feels like it takes us for ever to achieve them. We all sit at home and wait for Garry to walk through the door as if he's been to his head office in Coventry for meetings, which we know will never happen.

Amy suffers terrible flashbacks of that night. Zoe and Danielle also do but as they are slightly older they tend to go in quiet moods sitting alone. As regards to myself, I am completely broken-hearted. I am still off work. Taking medication to help me through the day. Sleepless nights just seeing him in intensive care. I can honestly say that, if it wasn't for my three girls, I do not want to live without Garry. It's too hard. My soulmate has gone and I just want to see and hear Garry. To have to turn off his life-support machine because of this needless and senseless act, I find hard to comprehend. To think that Garry recovered from stomach cancer 15 years ago and to be taken in such terrible circumstances . . . what is the point of everything?

Amy keeps asking why. When I took all the girls to visit him in hospital, her dad could not open his eyes. All Amy wanted was for her dad to open his eyes, so he could see that she was there. How do you tell your 13 year old that he will never open his eyes? All Amy sees in her mind is the picture of her dad being beaten to death and lying on the ground lifeless.

My family and friends have been wonderful. Their support network has been truly comforting to my girls and myself, without which we could not have coped. They have been by my side since that Friday night.

As far as I am concerned, life should mean life. After all, the tariff for murder is mandatory, but why, as the justice system does not uphold this sentence? There should be no lesser tariff, otherwise what is the point of it being mandatory?

Parents should take responsibility for their children. Garry and myself have brought up three girls together to respect other people and to be home, not walking the streets causing damage and intimidating other people by drinking and abusive language. What these people need to understand is that it could be their partners or parents that it happens to. Until this society stops thinking about number one, we should all try and pull together to stop these youth gangs going on rampages. Attacking people verbally and physically under the influence of drink and drugs does not, in any way, justify their actions. You do the crime, you must face the consequence and do the time. It is too easy to say, 'They are only children and there is nothing to do. What else can they do?' By society accepting this type of attitude from the youths gives out the wrong signals.

They should not be allowed to congregate on street corners under the bridges putting fear into people who simply want to just pass them by without any foul-mouth back chat to them. Parents have to face up to their responsibilities. Having children is unconditional and there is no time limit to it. If the children do not face up to the action, then we have to make the parent face the action.

By saying that they do not bother to turn up at court is simply passing the buck. Lock them up as well. A deterrent needs to be put into action. We have to make our streets safer to walk out on and not be afraid of retaliation. Until the government puts into place an effective deterrent, the youth of today know too well that they can get away with their actions.

Put them in the army for a certain length of time. If they have plenty of aggression, do it through boot camp. For far, far too long now, we have just given them a slap on the wrist and they now know the law better than most decent, hard-working people do.

To have prevented Garry's death would have been for the police to have acted before this incident. Plenty of police presence warning the youngsters away from our residential street. Instead, they are asked to empty their alcohol and given a stop warning. As soon as they turn their backs, they then go back and drink and smoke more from their hidden stash. Alcohol needs to be addressed as soon as possible.

For all too long, youngsters have been drinking and smoking into the early hours and then deciding to do acts of criminal damage and beat people up as a joke because of their influence by drink and drugs. A closer eye is needed on shopkeepers. Girls are becoming more violent than the boys.

When I finished, I took questions and described exactly how it was for me, as a mum, to sit in court and not be able to be near my girls as they went through the process of giving evidence. I described the sleepless nights, the tears, the upset and the anger that we'd all gone through, and how disgusted we were to find out that Swellings was in breach of bail conditions when he murdered Garry. He'd been in court that day on a charge of intimidation and had been specifically told by a magistrate to keep out of Warrington. He ignored that, like the arrogant young man he is, and went on to gang up with his mates in Warrington, get drunk and cause mayhem and murder. Why he was given bail in the first place was, and still is, completely beyond me. It was a decision that cost Garry his life. I also said publicly that I wished I'd never asked Garry to find out what was going on outside our house that evening, telling the press that I used to believe in the right to defend property until this happened to us. 'It's not worth it,' I added. 'It's far too high a price to pay.'

When I first spoke, I felt choked up, but as I answered questions I began to find an inner strength that I'd not known for many weeks. I'd sat in court, in silence, for a long time and now it was my turn to let go. I didn't realise I had so much that I wanted to say.

Little did I know that this statement would start the ball rolling in terms of the work I do now. I was still a victim, yes, but one who had a voice, and I felt like I was speaking up for many victims who have been through a court process I feel is weighted heavily in favour of defendants. I couldn't put it into so many words then, but by the end of the press conference I felt something had changed – not just for me, but for everyone who had ever suffered the effects of anti-social behaviour, however major or minor it was. At last, I felt we had a voice, and one that would not be so easily silenced from now on.

TWELVE

Speaking Out

Sentencing of the three youths convicted of Garry's murder was set for Monday, 11 February. This meant more waiting while pre-sentence reports and other documentation were prepared. I knew that the penalty for murder was a mandatory life sentence but I also knew that, in the British justice system, life does not mean life. As I'd said in my post-verdict statement, I believe it should be otherwise.

I certainly wasn't alone in my view. After my statement, the letters poured in once again from men and women all over the country, perhaps double the number that I'd received soon after Garry's murder.

Your speech at the press conference was outstanding, and just showed what ordinary decent people you are, like many others in this country who deplore the state of society. We shall continue to pester our MP until Parliament wakes up to its inability to protect society.

Your tragedy has touched our hearts. Let us hope your terrible loss will make a difference – please don't give up the fight to make our streets safer. The politicians must listen to the decent people of this country.

Your husband was a hero, he challenged the troublemakers of our society. Nowadays, few people are bothered to confront the culprits. Our society's standards have been going down for the last few years. I am glad to know you are going to campaign to improve our society and I would like to give my full support for this cause.

Campaign? This last letter got me thinking. I hadn't envisaged any campaigning. All I'd done was highlight some of the problems that many people faced in terms of anti-social behaviour, and how I thought we'd been let down by a system that I felt was weighted in favour of the defendant. I wanted the politicians to do something about it. Up to that point, I felt I was powerless to make big changes, but so many letters on a similar theme couldn't be ignored. Had I struck a deep chord and, if I had, what – if anything – could I do to follow up on such sentiments?

It was a passing thought, I have to admit. My main focus was getting us all through the next three weeks to the date of the sentencing. I knew they would be going to prison – of that there was no doubt – but for how long? I knew their ages would work in their favour, and the police made it very clear to me that, whatever sentence they got, they were likely to appeal it immediately. When you hear those words, you look at the legal team and police officers and think, 'When is this wheel going to be steered by the victims' families?' But your brain sends signals through your body and you smile respectfully and shake your head and go with the flow.

So all the family trooped back into Chester Crown Court on 11 February to see Swellings, Sorton and Cunliffe get their just deserts, or at least I hoped so.

Mr Justice Smith spoke very movingly about Garry. He said, 'When his wife's car had been damaged, Garry Newlove went out to find out what was happening. He did so because his family and wife were upset.

'These were the actions of a courageous and devoted family man, who paid with his life.

'The attack was seen by Garry Newlove's three daughters. They did all anyone could have done to help. Nobody who saw them during the trial could fail to have been touched and impressed by their simple and straightforward decency. I can't find a better word for it.'

The judge's words set me off crying. Everything I'd bottled up during the trial was now coming out. Thank God the family were around to support us.

As I wept, the judge turned to the dock. 'You were three of a gang who attacked Garry Newlove only because he had the courage to remonstrate with you. For you all, drunken aggression was part of the night's entertainment.

'Each of you continued to behave aggressively once you had finished with Garry Newlove. His teenage daughters saw him attacked and fatally injured and I must consider the effect on them and Mrs Newlove after such tough times.'

The judge sentenced Swellings to a minimum of 17 years in jail, Sorton to a minimum of 15 years and Cunliffe a minimum of 12 years. They stood there with their hands in their pockets. As far as I could see, they showed no remorse as they stood in the dock. There was the usual wailing from their families, but as far as I'm concerned they were crocodile tears. There was no doubt they would appeal for more lenient sentences and, besides, there would be time off for good behaviour. It sickens me even today to think they'll be getting ready to come out in just a few short years' time. Meanwhile, our sentence is for life.

Did we get justice for Garry? Not really. Justice is when the victim can walk back through the door, and that was obviously not going to happen. But I feel we did the best we could, and, while two of the five walked free, at least three of them were convicted. The whole process sickened me in that our witnesses, including my girls, were prodded and provoked into giving evidence that would cast doubt on the defendants' guilt. Yes, I believe in the concept of a fair trial and of course defendants have to be heard like anyone else. We were lucky, too, that we had a judge who was respectful and understanding towards us. Other than that, I often felt it was the Newlove family on trial, not Swellings, Sorton or Cunliffe.

For example, one day an adjournment was called because the prison van carrying one of the defendants (Sorton) was late. A defendant has a right to be offered refreshments while travelling down to court if they are delayed. Sorton declined refreshments on the way, but, as soon as we got into court, he changed his mind and demanded them because it was his 'right'. So another adjournment was called.

Then we had people saying all sorts of things within earshot of us. I remember two social workers behind me talking about some piece of evidence the prosecution had given. One of the social workers said, 'How do you know he [one of the defendants] said that?' When our family liaison officer turned round and said, 'Do you mind?', the social worker answered, 'And who are you?'

It was that sort of thing, and being in close proximity to the defendants' families, that drove me mad. We started taking our own lunch in because there was only one canteen in the court for all to use. This is not unusual – in fact, it is the case in all court buildings – but we found it to be a volatile situation when my family had to go into it. They couldn't stand the whispering and dirty looks thrown at them by the defendants' families and friends when they nipped down to the canteen for a piece of toast and a brew in the mornings. Of course, the legal teams for both sides had an area where they could sit and so were isolated from such intimidation. The witness-support staff were fantastic. They found a room for all of us to go into, but this wasn't a dedicated room for victims' families. It was a witness video-link room and we had to leave it when it was needed for another trial. It meant that, when the court needed to be cleared, we had to stand in the same corridor as the other families, which wasn't pleasant.

As was pointed out to me by one member of our legal team, the law in this country is a 'blunt tool' in that it is deemed better to let a guilty person go than to lock up an innocent person. Fair enough, but it does mean the system protects the defendant at all costs. As a family, we were ripped into and made to feel dirty. It made me very angry indeed, but I'm also glad that we managed to keep our dignity intact during the trial. It would've been so easy to start yelling and screaming at the defendants like a lot of victims' families do, emotionally drained and out of sheer frustration more than anything else. Since Garry's murder, I've met so many families who have been through the courts process as victims and have exactly the same stories as us. Surely that says something about the state of British justice and the legal system as it stands?

This leads me on to something I said to *The Sun* just after the three had been convicted. I was quoted as saying that we 'ought to think' about reintroducing the death penalty because 'it's the only way these kids are going to wake up to the pain they're causing'. I went on to say that I would be happy to witness their execution.

Now, I realise that these are shocking remarks and they've been thrown back at me time and time again in the years since Garry's murder. All I would say to those who have accused me of being cruel and callous, or have told me that my opinion makes me as bad as them, is this: try being in my shoes, or my daughters' shoes, and you might get some idea of the emotions I was going through when I said those words. It's easy for people to be kind and liberal when they're looking at a murder dispassionately, but I challenge anyone to go through what I've been through and not allow those thoughts to enter your head. Which is why I don't apologise for the remarks I made then. They were what they were, and if people can't understand the emotion and devastation that caused me to make them, that's their problem. I only hope they never find themselves in a similar situation.

Anyway, the remarks had been made and, once again, a flood of letters arrived at my house, almost all in support of what I'd said. These were the only comments I'd made to the press at the time, aside from the press conference, of course, which prompted acres of media coverage. I didn't read much of it, dazed as I was from the aftermath of the trial and knowing the sentencing was still to come, but Cheshire Police press office eventually presented me with a file full of photocopied clippings. Looking back now, I see how I somehow managed to capture public outrage at on-going anti-social behaviour and the problems caused by cheap alcohol. If newspapers are meant to reflect what their readers are thinking, it was clear I'd touched a nerve.

The *Manchester Evening News* reported:

Mrs Newlove spoke plainly and with amazing clarity in the aftermath of the verdicts, and covered all bases in the debate – curtailing the availability of cheap alcohol, emphasising parental responsibility and even creating boot camps were mentioned as ways of tackling the sheer loutish behaviour that strikes fear into ordinary people. We salute her courage in speaking out.

While the *News of the World* commented:

Brave Helen Newlove spoke for the nation this week with her powerful condemnation of the drunken youths who kicked husband Garry to death. We support all she said about parents accepting responsibility for their children and what is wrong with Britain's thuggish, feral underclass. Every politician should carry a copy of her speech.

There was blanket coverage of my speech in most of the national newspapers, as well as the ones local to Warrington, and everyone agreed my remarks had reflected a lot of public anger. But I was still just one person. What could I do to make real changes? Like many other people, I'd always voted in the hope that I'd see politicians making a difference. Usually I was disappointed, but it didn't stop me believing in democracy. I always assumed, like everyone else, that it takes many people to make a difference, and that the wheels of change, particularly in Parliament, move very slowly.

Besides, I had my life to get on with. Swellings, Sorton and Cunliffe were behind bars, and, while there was no doubt that they would appeal, we knew that, for the moment, they were safely under lock and key.

After the sentencing, I had agreed to be interviewed on GMTV. But I wanted us to go on as a family. If this was going to keep attracting such media interest, the girls were as much a part of the story as I was and I felt it was right they should speak for themselves. Previously, I'd not wanted any media contact with them. Our lives had been shattered and just getting enough energy to see us through the day was our main focus, nothing else. But GMTV was familiar to us all, as I'd watched it as the girls were growing up. Although I'd never met any of them, there was something homely and safe about the presenting team. I knew they wouldn't be harsh with us – well, I hoped so.

We were collected from home by Elaine Wilcox, a reporter on the morning show, and we all travelled down to London together. Elaine was lovely to us all and we are still in touch as she lives in the north-west. We arrived just before midnight, and were put up in a hotel for two nights. After all we'd been through, it felt like a bit of a treat, even though we were all still in 'la-la land', as I now call it. The hotel was really posh and the girls almost felt like their old selves. Then their faces would switch off and they would go silent.

I hadn't been to London since I was ten, and was amazed at all the changes that had happened there. Little did I know then how much London would become part of my life.

The next morning, Elaine had arranged to do some pre-filming, which would be shown before we did our interview live on the sofa the next day. When everything for the interview had been finalised, the girls wanted to have a look around the shops but I just wanted to lie down. They begged me to let them go out so I did – once I'd made sure they were contactable at all times.

That evening, we had dinner and snuggled down for the night. Amy was staying in my room, with Danielle and Zoe next door.

We were driven to the studios very early the following day. Zoe and Danielle were excited and in good spirits but Amy had been upset the night before, and had become quiet and withdrawn. She was very pale, and the closer our interview slot came, the more sick and scared she looked. In the end, I asked her if she really wanted to do it.

'No, Mum,' she said, 'I feel too nervous and I don't want to say the wrong thing. Is it all right if I don't do it?'

Of course it was all right, so Amy waited in the Green Room while we had our make-up done and got ready to go on live TV. Walking down to the studio didn't seem real but Fiona Phillips, the interviewer, really put us at our ease. As I told her what impact Garry's death had had on us as a family, I could see she had tears in her eyes and it was as much as I could do not to cry as well. Zoe and Danielle were brilliant, and they just talked about their dad in a natural, honest and unaffected way. I remember Zoe saying that no one should ever have to go through what they'd been through, while Danielle described the effect Garry's death had had on Amy.

'It is just not the same; Amy is completely different,' she said. 'She doesn't know who she is at the moment. She was always with her dad and messing about, joking about, being sarcastic.'

Much later on, Fiona Phillips said that she'd come close to breaking down after she'd met us, and that she'd been so choked up she could barely carry out the next interview. The sight of me holding Garry's glasses and T-shirt – items I took everywhere with me – while she talked to us really upset her, and she said it had been one of the most memorable encounters she'd ever had – and she's met a lot of people.

I can't say it was an enjoyable interview, but it was nice to get away from the north-west for a day or so, and we were pleased we'd been invited on and managed to get through well enough.

We all went back home, still feeling shell-shocked and wondering why the hell our lives had been turned inside out so completely over the past six months.

My sister Marie was staying with us while we tried to pick up the pieces and attempted to restore some kind of normality. One morning, I switched on the TV and flicked over to *Sky News*, where an American called Sergio Argueta was being interviewed about gang violence. He said he was sick of attending the funerals of friends affected by gang violence, which is why he'd set up an organisation to try to educate young people about the dangers of gangs. He said the first step to change began with a refusal to engage in negative behaviour.

'I agree with everything he's saying,' I said to Marie as we watched him. 'He's got it spot on.'

'Why don't you email in to tell him then?' Marie replied.

'Oh, I don't know if I should,' I said. 'They might think I'm being daft.'

'No, they won't. Just do it.'

Well, I had nothing to lose and, since so many people had been supportive of me, I thought it would be good to give something back. I switched on the computer and emailed the address that was rolling across the screen, asking for comments. I said who I was, and that I had also been the victim of gang violence.

We carried on watching the telly. The interview finished and some other news item began. Then I let out a scream: my name was being flashed up. 'Breaking news: Garry Newlove's widow supports anti-gang campaigner,' it said, or something like that. We stared at it open-mouthed, unable to believe that my words had made the TV so quickly.

Five minutes later, the phone rang.

'Hi, Helen.' It was Jackie, the press officer at Cheshire Police who'd been so helpful to us over the last few months. She sounded shocked. 'Helen, what have you done?' she said. 'I've a pile of media interview requests for you here, and I've been telling them to hang on while you recover from the trial. Next thing is, you pop up on *Sky News*!'

'Oh, God,' I said. 'I'm really sorry. I didn't think that would happen.'

She started to laugh. 'My phone's going as I speak,' she said. 'I'll have to take down some of these numbers and call you back.'

I put the phone down and turned to Marie. 'I knew it would be daft,' I said. 'I've really let the genie out of the bottle now.'

'Stop worrying,' she said, 'and let's see who wants to talk to you first.'

In a day or two, we received the full list from Jackie. Almost all the national newspapers, loads of women's magazines and half a dozen TV programmes wanted me to speak to them. I was overwhelmed by requests and it was hard to know which to pick.

Although I'd had no media training, the GMTV interview gave me the confidence to consider other interviews. However, I was still wary. So far, the media had been very good and respectful towards us, but I wasn't daft enough to think that such a situation wouldn't change. I'd seen how the press turned on people they'd previously been friends with and it bothered me that, in time, we would become their victims too. I decided that if I was going to do some interviews I would ask my dearest friend, Tina, and her partner, Gary, to make contact with the journalists first and, if they felt comfortable, I would agree to meet them.

That way, I ended up doing quite a bit of work with *The Sun* and the *News of the World*. I trusted Keith and Ben, the News International reporters I worked with. A lot has been said about the tabloids since, particularly the *News of the World*, of course, but I have to say that whatever I told them was reported fairly and accurately.

One of the first interviews I did came out not long after Garry's murderers were sentenced. In it, I said that bar managers and licensees who sell alcohol to minors should be banned from the trade for life. I also called for a ban on alcopops and legislation to force TV companies to show less binge drinking on programmes that appealed to teenagers.

'Every time you turn on the TV, you see a soap set in a bar or club. *Coronation Street* and *EastEnders* revolve around pubs. *Hollyoaks* constantly features boozing teenagers,' I said. 'The end result is that kids are totally acclimatised to alcohol. They can't draw the line between TV and reality and so grow up thinking it's cool and normal to get hammered.'

I added that, while I thought Garry's killers would've done what they did anyway, the effect of alcohol gave thugs like them the Dutch courage to go out and behave badly.

I just wanted answers from an industry that seemed to thrive on youngsters throwing drink down themselves without knowing their limits, or anyone telling them that enough is enough. I couldn't understand how such behaviour had become a normal part of everyday life, and why parents were allowing their children to go out and drink in this way. Surely I wasn't alone in thinking that young people drinking themselves unconscious, or into a whole lot of trouble, was just wrong?

I didn't know what I could do, but I wanted to do something. The media seemed to sense that and I was asked by a number of organisations whether I wanted to get involved in various projects. In those first few weeks, it was hard to know which to accept and which to reject, as I had no media advisers and little experience of how it all worked. However, the one that appealed the most was an offer from Channel 4's *Dispatches* documentary programme, which would follow me meeting politicians, police officers, victims of crime and young offenders to find answers to the problems of youth crime. I knew *Dispatches* made hard-hitting documentaries and I didn't want to pull any punches in my dealings with people. In truth, I was looking for answers to what had happened to me.

I went all over the place with the production team and felt comfortable with the process. Mind you, it wasn't without its difficulties. We went to one estate where I interviewed a guy who'd tried to turn things around, and as we were talking on camera a gang of lads surrounded him and started kicking footballs in his direction. The situation became volatile and we were forced to leave.

I also interviewed Jack Straw MP, who was then Secretary of State for Justice. Now, some time around this period – and

I apologise if my memory is sometimes a blur, as there was so much going on at that time – I was invited to talk to MPs at a Commons Select Committee on policing in the 21st century. My contribution concerned the court process and, as you might expect, I gave them both barrels. I said it was totally disgusting how victims were treated in court and the legal system.

'As victims in court, we want more help and respect,' I said. 'You go in the court with all the emotions, and then you are fighting for a seat. The press have a box, the legal people have a box, but there is no respect for the families.

'You do not know who you are sitting next to. I think it's utterly disgraceful because you think that the courts are for you, that they are your safety net.'

I also argued that smaller police stations should not close in favour of larger, more centralised ones where officers were bogged down in paperwork. I said that kids knew that there were fewer bobbies on the beat, who wouldn't come out unless absolutely necessary, and that this had led to Garry's death.

It appeared that Jack Straw had picked up on what I'd said because the night before I was due to interview him I received an email from his office. It had a letter attached, addressed to me. In it, Mr Straw pretty much accused me of having a go at the trial judge in Garry's case. He also said that Chester Crown Court was a historic court and that it couldn't possibly meet all the demands of victims' families. He said he'd checked with the clerk of the court, and discovered we'd been given a room and witness support. This was all true, but it didn't mean it was perfect, and it certainly didn't mean that the situation for victims' families couldn't improve. He took everything I said to the Select Committee as a negative, which it wasn't meant to be. I read the letter and thought, 'How dare you?' The people who dealt with us in court were fantastic, but they were running on a shoestring and it was up to the government to change that. I felt he was patronising me, but if this letter was an attempt to throw me off asking tough questions he was very much mistaken.

We did the interview about the criminal justice system and not once did I mention the letter. 'You can ask me,' I thought.

During a break in filming, he brought up the subject and I told him I thought he had been rude and patronising. 'Instead of going behind my back, why didn't you just ask me about the trial?' I said. 'Why did you have to send a letter?'

He fiddled with his tie, looking nervous, and seemed quite shocked that I had the nerve to tackle him. I thought, 'I wish you had just spoken to me first and found out what I really meant and we could have moved on.' I would have thought more of him if he had not jumped to conclusions and thought I was attacking him. I wanted everyone, including politicians, to understand the bad experiences victims endure, so together we could try to make things better. My criticisms of the system were all made so that we could have a better deal for other victims. It was never just negative whinging. David Cameron got it, Jack Straw obviously didn't. His advisers and press people were around looking slightly apprehensive, but that didn't bother me. MPs are elected to serve the people, and as one of those people you're entitled to have your say when you meet them. Anyway, I think the message hit home because the next time I met him he was all smiles.

Quite a bit of the documentary was about meeting young lads who'd offended or were being rehabilitated in the community. I wanted to know how they felt about what they'd done, and whether imprisonment had worked for them. Some of the lads had breached their parole conditions and were back inside for an extra bit of time. They were interested in what had happened to me and I was keen to tell them. By and large, they were appalled by what had happened and seemed to understand the impact it had had on us as a family. But some of them couldn't change their own behaviour, and I found that rather sad. There were some who found the transition from prison too difficult and actually wanted to be back inside. What I concluded was there are no clear guidelines or strategies in place when it comes to dealing with young offenders. Their treatment was piecemeal and often confusing. Like the courts system, everything was on a budget and young offenders' programmes weren't really working. For example, I came across one group of lads cleaning plaques on a pier. What was the point of that? Teach them a skill they can use!

Part of the journey of the programme took me to Hackney where I met a wonderful young man called Nathan Levy. When I went to meet him outside Hackney Town Hall, he was sitting on a beautiful white marble bench that was dedicated to his younger brother Robert Levy, who was stabbed to death in London in 2004 aged just 16. Nathan and I got on very well. He told me about the night of Robert's murder and the sadness and pain that his family went through. What struck me about Nathan and how he spoke about his family was the dignity with which they held themselves together. Nathan and I have met several times since, and, even now, when I think about our first meeting, I feel such warmth inside me. Nathan's parents Ian and Pat are truly remarkable people. I love and respect them dearly for all the selfless acts that they carry out daily to give the young people of Hackney a better chance in life through the Robert Levy Foundation. Nathan talked about a charity called Through Unity, which supports families who have been bereaved as a result of youth violence. He told me about their Chief Executive, civil servant Rani King, and suggested I should meet her. Rani had helped Nathan's father and Richard Taylor set it up. Richard was the father of ten-year-old schoolboy Damilola, who had been stabbed to death by two teenagers in 2000.

In time, I would meet Rani, but little did I know how much help she would give me and what she would come to mean to me. The girls and I first met Rani at the appeals court. Nathan had promised to be with us, but it had brought back so many bad memories of his own family's agony that he could not walk through the doors, and he called Rani to step in for him. She rushed to my side to support me and has just stayed there as part of the family. She may be retired now, but she doesn't slow down and she is one of the warmest and most giving people I've ever had the pleasure to meet.

The finished film came out that summer. It was well received – by my own family, as well as TV viewers – but I wasn't all that happy with the way it was edited. It portrayed me as the victim, looking at pictures of Garry and reading cards, then packing up the house ready to move. I wanted it to be edgier, and to concentrate on the issues, not on the person who was instigating the debate. Anyway, the programme had at least raised some of the issues I was becoming passionate about and it was a learning curve for me. It was to be the first of many.

THIRTEEN

New Beginnings

As the *Dispatches* film had shown, we were moving house. Nice as the house was, I didn't want to rent any more and I felt it was important that the girls had a place they could call their own. Although I still owned our house in Station Road North, I couldn't and wouldn't go back there. Nor did I want to sell it, so renting it out was the only option.

I couldn't decide whether to stay in the Warrington area or leave it altogether. My parents were still there, of course, and I wanted to be near them, but the place was tainted with memories of what had happened to Garry. My best friend Tina lives in Buxton and I'd always loved the place. I began to wonder what it would be like if we moved there, and if I had been on my own I wouldn't have thought twice about it. But the girls had just lost their dad; they didn't want to lose their friends too. So I left it up to them and they elected to stay around Warrington. 'Fair enough,' I thought. 'They've been through too much to cope with a big move.' I only found out recently that Amy wouldn't have minded going to Buxton, but the other two said, 'You tell Mum we don't want to go'! In the end, we stayed.

I also had to make a big decision about work. The Manchester law firm I worked for, Berg and Co, had been terrific with me, keeping me on full pay until I was ready to decide what to do. In the spring after the trial, they wrote to me and said that, while they understood how hard it was, we had to come to a decision about my job. Did I want to return to work?

I thought about it, and said 'no'. I couldn't go back. I'd come home from work on the Friday Garry was murdered and I couldn't imagine getting up one Monday morning and going in for the first day back, like nothing had happened. In the intervening months, almost every aspect of my life had changed. I wasn't sure I could sit in an office, wading through contracts and arguments and this, that and the other without thinking, 'What am I doing here?' It wasn't fair on them, so I allowed Berg to let me go. I'd put in for criminal injuries compensation, which I knew wouldn't go far, but, when you're in la-la land, like I was then, you just live for the day. Looking back, I spent money on the girls to make their lives more comfortable, giving them things that would bring a smile to their faces. I felt – and still feel – that I had let them down as a mother. I wanted to wrap them up in cotton wool and protect them from all sorrow and pain. Buying things was my comfort blanket around them.

For example, after the trial we went on a family holiday to Barbados. Garry and I had planned to go there for our silver wedding anniversary, but as that wasn't going to happen I decided to take the girls. It was a disaster. Yes, it was a beautiful place, but it just wasn't the same without him. I had a panic attack the moment I arrived and I felt wobbly for the next fortnight. We were all ill with stomach upsets and Amy was severely sunburned. The girls were always hearing the shouts of 'Dad! Dad!' from other kids on the beach and I was constantly asked where my husband was. In short, we were relieved to get back to Warrington. Never mind, we'd tried, and perhaps it did us good to get out of the environment for a while. My family had warned me that it was a big trip after such a traumatic experience, but I thought we could handle it. There were other similar lessons to be learned in our new lives.

The girls were still not back at school. They did try, because they didn't want to be apart from their friends, but it was very difficult. No one really knew what to say when they did turn up, and it upset them to hear other pupils moaning about their parents. They understood that most kids were living normal lives and they weren't, but it was still hard. Danielle took her GCSEs but she didn't get the results she would have obtained otherwise. She did her best in the circumstances and I admire her for that.

When we moved into the new house, Amy decided she wanted to return to school and, although it was sometimes a battle, she got up every morning, walked there and faced whatever the day brought. Then one day she came home looking upset. When I asked her what was the matter, she told me that her GCSE law class had been looking at criminal law – murder cases. They were asked to look on the internet at previous cases and her dad's case had appeared on Google. Of course, that set her back but she did not want to make a scene in school. The teacher realised something was up and approached her to see if she was having problems. She told me, 'I don't know who felt the worst, Mum. As you know, I don't like anyone to fuss over me.' And so she ended up sympathising with her teacher, who was new to the school and didn't know what had happened.

'Miss, it's all right. Don't worry, these things happen,' Amy had said to her.

And so that is how Amy handled such situations and somehow got through her last year in school.

When it was Amy's last day, I took some flowers in for a teacher who'd really supported her, and me. She said Amy was an inspiration.

'There were times I'd come into work in a bad mood,' she

said, 'then I'd see Amy smiling and I'd think, "What have I got to moan about?"'

Amy stuck it out, her dry sense of humour pulling her through some of the tougher moments at school, and she did really well. Good on her for her determination to succeed. She's made me very proud.

At the time of Garry's death, Zoe was considering university and we'd been up to the University of Central Lancashire in Preston to have a look round. She was offered a place and, to her credit, did eventually start her course in the October. Sadly, someone recognised her name and word soon went round that she was Garry's daughter. The local and student press bombarded her with requests for interviews until the police were forced to intervene. After that, she lost interest and she left within a few weeks. 'I can't do it,' she said. 'It's just too difficult. I remember going up with you and Dad, and it's not the same now.'

Her mind would just switch off. She had the talent but how do you cope with all the grief inside you at the same time? University life is hard to get into under normal circumstances, but in Zoe's case there was no formula and no sticking plasters big enough to get her through. The tutors were very understanding but Zoe did not have the energy any more.

I understood, and I wasn't going to put pressure on her. She eventually got a job in the Trafford Centre in Manchester and now she's a successful make-up artist. I think she'll go back and do that degree one day but only when the time is right for her.

Grieving is a huge process and we're still doing it. People have said that therapy can help and I'm sure it can, but they didn't want it and, in a way, we've all been one another's therapists. However, I have to say that we have received help from another source, and, unusual as it might seem, it is something that has given us great comfort and support.

I've mentioned that I grew up in a strict Roman Catholic

household and, while I've not really been the best example of a Catholic over the years, I haven't neglected the spiritual side of life. I am a firm believer in heaven and hell. I truly believe that you will be called to account to justify your life on this earth. It is a simple philosophy but it is what I believe. I teach my girls right from wrong because I believe there is a greater being who sees everything we do. My faith is very strong in that. I also believe in an after-life and I'm convinced that our spirit stays around for some time after death. Some of the experiences I've had seem to bear this out.

Some years ago, I read Gloria Hunniford's book about her daughter, Caron Keating, and found it very moving. I was touched by the way she wrote about Caron's illness and subsequent death, and how she coped in the aftermath. But what really caught my interest was the fact that she often finds feathers in unusual places, where no birds could possibly be, and takes it as a sign of her daughter's continuing communication with this world.

I remember telling Garry about it, saying that if I died first I would send him a feather to show him I was still around. Garry being Garry, he treated it as a big joke.

'What do you mean?' he'd said and laughed. 'Are you saying you'll come back to haunt me?'

'No,' I said, 'I'm serious. I think it's a nice thing to do. It's not scary.'

As I sat by his bedside on the night he was attacked, I thought about the promise I'd made to Garry. It was impossible to believe that he was in this place, hovering between life and death. I put my head on his pillow and whispered in his ear.

'Garry,' I said, 'if you leave us, let me know you're still around. I know you laughed at me, but please send me a white feather to say you are still around and looking after us.'

Even then I felt daft saying it, but I meant it. After he died,

I was too caught up in my grief, and that of the girls, to start looking for any signs of an after-life. But right at the very end of the trial, when we were sitting out those long hours waiting for the jury's decision, I noticed two small white feathers on the carpet near my feet. The room was one used for giving video evidence and there was no way two feathers could have got in there. I didn't say anything, thinking it was probably my imagination working overtime. A few moments later, some of our family came up from a room downstairs. Marie told me that as they stood around chatting, three white feathers floated down from above. Again, no sign of any birds, or any other physical way they could have appeared. It affected me deeply. I didn't have time to rationalise it then but I felt that a message was being sent; by whom I don't know, but it made me feel calm.

We were called back into court to hear the verdicts – three convicted and two acquitted. Now, I like logical explanations for everything, but I couldn't find a single one for this. Pure coincidence? Maybe, but where did those feathers come from in the first place?

Since then, I've come across small white feathers in the most unlikely of places and I know it's a sign that Garry is around, and still watching over us. I've trusted the most sensible people with this information and, while they've probably thought I was daft at the time, they've changed their minds when they too have seen the same feathers.

Whatever the explanation, the appearance of the feathers from time to time has given me great comfort. Mitch Winehouse, Amy Winehouse's dad, recounts similar events involving butterflies and birds. It seems to be a regular occurrence for people whose loved ones have passed on. Of course, cynics will discount these experiences as wishful thinking or even think that you've lost your marbles. But I say, 'Don't mock what you don't know,' and there are greater things like miracles for which science has no rational explanation. If it doesn't hurt anyone, people shouldn't be so quick to judge. It wouldn't surprise me, knowing Garry's sense of humour, if he is sitting up there on his cloud with some poor bald bird, plucking it to send me the messages I so badly need. He will be laughing as he does it.

I still have my Catholic faith and reading the Bible soon after Garry's death was also a comfort. To be honest, though, I've questioned the Church's teachings since it happened, even though I'm still a believer. I've only been to church once since Garry's funeral and it was very emotional indeed. I haven't been back.

We cope with our loss in the best way we can. We talk to one another, and give one another space too. Many families shut themselves off from their feelings, or try to push it all aside, but we're not like that and I'm glad. I hope my girls can talk to me about anything and everything and, although we're often private with other people, within our family group we are open and I'd like it to stay that way. There are many times when, as a mum, I wish I could carry their burden too. I'm sure all parents know how that feels.

Anyway, aside from the feathers, we had more earthly matters to concentrate on. After the *Dispatches* programme, I did some interviews for women's magazines and I was often asked how I'd like Garry to be remembered. It wasn't something I'd given a lot of thought to, but when I did mull it over I realised that I would like to lend his name to something worthwhile. However, I just couldn't decide what that would be, even though various people said it would be a great idea to create 'something big' in his honour.

Around the same time, Zoe was contacted by the Warrington Wolves Foundation, a charity connected to the famous rugby league team in our town. Their aim was to engage young people and help them out via sport and promoting healthy lifestyles. I had done a magazine interview in which I spoke about wanting better opportunities for young people, and the Foundation had picked up on that. Somehow they had tracked down Zoe, and they asked her to come and see what they were doing with local young people. She accepted their offer after talking it through with me. I encouraged her to go as I felt it would be good for her to see something positive around young people.

Zoe was blown away by what she saw. She was deeply impressed by the way the Foundation reached out not only to young people but also to the whole community. They run all sorts of clubs and activity sessions, including dance classes, creative arts, yoga and, of course, rugby coaching sessions. Zoe found the kids involved to be happy and healthy, enjoying all that the Foundation had put in place for them.

'Mum, it was brilliant,' she enthused when she got home. 'We should try and do something like that, or just join in with what they're doing.'

Although Garry was never a rugby fan, I was impressed enough by Zoe's response to go and have a look for myself, and I was also amazed by the amount of good work they were doing. I knew then that Zoe was right and, perhaps with the support of Warrington Wolves Foundation, we should set something up to honour Garry Newlove the man, not the murder victim.

However, by this time we had other things to contend with. Swellings and Sorton had both lodged appeals against their sentences. I'd been warned at the time of their sentencing that they would do this and I wasn't surprised, given what I knew of the legal system. Of course, it protects their right to appeal but it doesn't give the victim any say in that. I vowed I would be there in person when the appeal hearing took place, come what may.

More importantly, it was coming up to the first anniversary

of Garry's death. Warrington Borough Council contacted me via a third party to see if I would consider a memorial service for Garry on the anniversary of his death. The letter was a respectful one and, after talking it over with the girls, we decided it would be a good idea. There had been a candlelit vigil for Garry a week after his death, as I've described, but, of course, none of us felt up to attending that. A year on, a memorial service felt like it would be closure, to some extent, of our time in that area and also a good way for local people to show their support for us, which I knew they were continuing to do. After some discussion, we decided to have a service at Christ Church in Padgate, where Garry's funeral was held, followed by a candlelit procession to Station Road North.

The days leading up to the event were emotional yet calming at the same time. Knowing that the community wanted to pay their respects to Garry meant a great deal to us and it showed they remembered him. The weather was horrendous that day; it just poured down but, again, the church was packed. Even the crowd of media people were respectful and subdued. Garry's death had prompted a feeling of unity and support. I truly felt people recognised it could have happened to them or their loved ones. It became very personal and there was a huge wave of compassion and support for us. Around 200 people came, mostly locals, and it was nice to see a few familiar faces again. The girls and I decided that it would be lovely to light a candle on the spot where Garry had fallen. So, after the service, everyone followed us, collected candles and lit them after a few prayers were spoken by the vicar. I recollect saying to the girls that their dad would have joked, 'Look at you lot getting soaking wet through, and I'm lovely and dry,' as he dangled his legs over his cloud.

The girls had written such simple loving tributes to their father and I felt I had to read them out loud to those who had braved the terrible weather to stand with us.

'I get told time's a great healer,' Zoe said. 'I wish time could rewind itself so this person would see me graduate from university. I wish time would rewind so that he could walk me down the aisle. Accepting that he's not coming back is the hardest thing ever.'

'My dad never saw my 16th birthday, he never got to see me in my prom dress,' said Danielle.

Amy added, 'It hurts me to think what pain my dad went through on that night, but I think he feels more pain not to be with his family right now. He wasn't just my father, he was my best friend.'

I was very choked up as I read out their heartfelt words, so moving and honest, but at least I felt we had given Garry the honour he deserved.

FOURTEEN

Putting the Fun in Fundraising

After the emotion of the anniversary, our thoughts turned once more to setting up some kind of tribute to Garry. We wanted to bring in Garry's deep love of music and, taking inspiration from the Warrington Wolves Foundation, include something that would engage young people. We ummed and aahhed over a few ideas but couldn't come to a firm conclusion. Whatever we did, however, would need funds and we had to find a way of raising money. Quite quickly, we developed the idea of having some kind of one-off charity event – a dance or evening function with music – that would help to launch it.

I'd never done anything like that in my life, so I took the direct approach, emailing agents, managers, business people – anyone I could think of – who might be able to help. I discovered that Simon Moran was the owner of Warrington Wolves. What I didn't know then was that he was also one of the country's biggest concert promoters, putting on thousands of events every year including huge festivals. I was told that he was a nice guy but a very busy man, and not to expect a response quickly. Well, he did reply, almost by return email, saying he was very keen to help. Simon is a Warrington-born man and is passionate about his home town.

He said he'd have a think about an act or acts suitable for a charity event, and would also handle ticket sales. We could also hire a function room at Warrington Wolves rugby club and he'd give us advice about room decoration, sound, lighting, etc.

This was a great start for us, but I didn't quite realise what we'd put into motion until I got a call on my mobile a few days later. I was at the Trafford Centre with the girls, sitting in Pizza Hut. Now the ball was rolling, I was fretting a bit that people might not be very interested in the event and we wouldn't sell many tickets. It was playing on my mind, so we'd decided to get out of the house and go for some retail therapy.

'Hiya,' said the voice on the line. 'Is that 'Elen?'

'Yes,' I replied. I thought I recognised the voice but couldn't place it. 'Who's this?'

'It's Peter Kay. I wanted to 'ave a word about this charity do o' yours.'

Right. So Peter Kay's ringing me up while I'm in Pizza Hut. I wasn't falling for that one. It had to be one of my nephews winding me up.

'All right, soft lad,' I said, 'stop messing. I know it's you. Get off the phone, my pizza's going cold!'

'It's not a joke, honestly.' The voice laughed on the end of my phone. 'It *is* me, Peter Kay! I'm just driving home from Granada Studios and I thought I'd give you a call. Can you talk?'

I put my hand over the receiver. 'It's Peter Kay!' I whispered to the girls.

They started giggling and Amy shouted, 'Garlic bread!'

'Eh, I heard that,' Peter said. 'Who've you got there then?'

I told him it was my girls and he laughed. 'Cheeky buggers . . .' he said. 'Anyway, look, if you're busy I'll give you a call tonight. About nine. Is that all right?'

Well, we got home sharpish and Peter was as good as his

word, ringing on the dot of 9 p.m. I'd loved his humour for ages and I couldn't believe I was speaking to him.

'I thought it were terrible what happened to your Garry,' he said. 'I read about it and I was appalled. I'm a father myself. What happened to Garry should never have happened and I would like to support you and the girls.

'Your Garry sounded like a really nice man. If you want me to do something for this charity night, count me in. I tell you what, Helen − if I'd heard it was on and I didn't have an invite, I'd have gatecrashed it anyway.'

'Oh, that'd be great,' I said. 'Thanks so much for your help.'

I couldn't believe it − Britain's best comedian offering to help us. Of course I wanted him involved. He asked me who else I'd been in touch with, and I said, 'Simon Moran.'

'Simon Moran! Right, well, Simon Moran'll have to get his act together for you then. Do you know he's one of my best mates?'

I didn't, and I told him I was meeting Simon at Warrington Wolves the following Saturday.

'Hang on,' Peter said. 'I'll just check me diary.' He went off the line for a few seconds. 'Right,' he said, 'I'm free next Sat'day, so I'll come down too. Is that all right?'

That meeting gave me something to look forward to all week. All the girls wanted to come but I thought it might be a bit much if we turned up in force, so I just asked Zoe along.

I know we were meant to be talking business, but Peter had me in stitches that day. I had promised Zoe I wouldn't burst out laughing all the time and embarrass her, a promise I broke as soon as I'd shaken hands with him. He takes the mick mercilessly, and always gets away with it. By contrast, Simon is a quiet sort of guy, but you can tell there is a very sharp mind at work there. He wondered who else we could get for the event.

'How about Rick Astley?' Peter said. 'He's brilliant. And he's from Warrington. I bet he'd do it.'

'Oh, that'd be great,' I said. 'He was one of Garry's favourites.'

'Yeah, he is good,' agreed Zoe.

Peter turned to her, a broad grin on his face. 'Now, come on,' he said, laughing. 'You're not fooling anyone. You don't know who Rick Astley is, do you?'

'I do!' she protested. 'He's that singer. My dad liked him.'

'Yeah, yeah,' Peter said, 'don't come that. You were only a twinkle in your dad's eye when Rick were top of the pops!'

Zoe blushed and giggled.

'Leave Rick to me,' Peter said. 'I've been doing some work with him recently. I'm sure he'll help.'

Peter offered to compère the event. 'Whatever you want me to do, I'll do it,' he said.

'I've never organised anything like this before,' I replied. 'I don't know what I want you to do because I don't know what I'm doing myself.'

'You'll be all right,' Peter said. 'You're not shy.'

Well, he might be a sharp cookie but he couldn't have got it more wrong. I am very shy, and being married to Garry the extrovert for 21 years I didn't have to step into the limelight because he was there already.

However, I was still worried that, even with Peter and Rick, we wouldn't grab the public's attention enough to turn it into ticket sales. Simon assured me that it would work out, and that if the publicity was right we would do it. What we needed, he said, was a firm idea of what we would do with the money raised. We needed to come up with something – and that's how the Newlove Warrington Foundation was born.

As Garry had loved music, it had to be at the heart of whatever we did. After a few brainstorming sessions, we came up with the idea of a community radio station, run by young people, which would allow them to express themselves and also give them great experience. We'd purchase the equipment and lend it out to youth-based organisations that could make good use of it. We would also work closely with the Warrington Wolves Foundation to make the town a safer and better place to live for everyone. I wanted Garry to be remembered for who he was and what he did, not for the way he died, and I wanted people to recognise Warrington as a place where public-spirited people like Garry existed. The money raised from the charity event would go into creating the station and enable us to carry out community work in schools and youth organisations.

The gala evening was to be held on Saturday, 8 November 2008, at Warrington Wolves. Like anyone planning a major event, from a birthday bash to a wedding, I was very nervous as we counted down the days. I really began to think, 'Helen, what have you done?' There seemed to be so much to organise, but we had a huge amount of help from various individuals and organisations who promised to provide goods and services to make the evening a success. My biggest fear was still that the tickets wouldn't sell, and all our efforts would end in a big fat flop. Luckily, the local and regional press picked up on the story – and the involvement of the celebrities, of course – and by the time the evening was upon us I could've sold double the number. In fact, people were still ringing me up on the Saturday to see if I had any spares.

The room at the Halliwell Jones Stadium was spectacularly decorated and there were bottles and bottles of champagne, donated by Marks and Spencer. It is a very long room and I wanted everyone to feel engaged and intimate. We put TV screens around the room so that no one missed anything on the night. I wanted the wow factor but I didn't want to spend much money, so we draped the ceiling with black cloth with tiny stars of light. The tables were dressed with white tablecloths and fluted vases filled with flowers exuding beautiful aromas.

I wanted the girls to look stunning after all they had been through. They were in long formal gowns and looked absolutely beautiful. They wanted their dad to be proud. And that night they were radiant. Me being me, I was rushing around trying to make sure everything was right and that everyone was having a good time. I can't remember exactly what was on the menu, only that it was sumptuous, because I was too nervous to eat a bite.

Peter Kay naturally overshadowed everybody. He even took the mick out of the posh starter ('Ham hock? Ham hock? What's that when it's at 'ome?') and had the 400 or so guests in stitches all night. Rick Astley was excellent too, singing all his hits and really getting people going. He'd brought his own band members with him – probably eight in total. Towards the end of Rick's set, Peter teased him that he wouldn't be able to remember all the words to 'Never Gonna Give You Up'. 'You'll have to get the book out, Rick!' he shouted.

Not to be outdone, Rick invited Peter up to duet with him and the two of them provided a memorable end to a truly amazing evening.

That night, when I lay in bed going over the evening, one of the lasting thoughts I had was the simple charm of Peter, who was so down to earth. He did not have an ego and was quite happy to sit and chat to people in the cloakroom. When it got too much for the staff in there, he then exploded onto the stage so everyone could see him. It was a truly fitting launch for Newlove Warrington. His sense of humour was so like Garry's. I can't express in words how grateful I am to Simon, Peter, Rick and so many others who gave my family a purpose and a feeling that we could do something to keep Garry's name alive.

Of course, the evening wasn't just for fun. The main focus was raising money and we managed to collect £64,000 on the night. A fair bit of that had to go on costs, of course, but we'd done very well indeed and had made more than enough to launch the radio station project, which would be called Newlove FM. Gordon Burns, from the BBC's *Look North West*, interviewed Peter and me during the evening and Peter said how delighted and honoured he was to be involved. Then I spoke about the reasons for starting the campaign and what we hoped to achieve. I said it was about giving youngsters activities, instead of them saying, 'There's nothing to do,' and that this was about Garry Newlove the person, not the man who was murdered. While I was speaking, I noticed Peter watching me intently and I felt his mind ticking over, working out what to say next.

'Eh,' he said, when I'd finished, 'she's good, in't she? She's like Barack Obama!'

I had to laugh. Peter really made the night and he made sure that, while everyone knew why we were here and what had prompted it, a real sense of positivity was flowing through the room. God love him, you couldn't get him off the stage! Although our paths haven't crossed since, I hope he realises that that evening was the first step on a path that has led me to the House of Lords and to helping make changes. I hope we meet again so that I can thank him in person.

So it was a very successful evening, and there were some very positive developments following the event too; a company there that night donated two computers for us to use at Warrington Wolves Foundation, which had become our base. I was still very much feeling my way into this new role, arranging school visits and making contacts within the local council and other bodies to see where resources were needed and where we could help. And, according to the media company de Winter who gave me a hand with publicity, the pop-up station in the centre helped us reach over 4.5 million people in just two weeks and secure media coverage worth over £120,000.

Unfortunately, after such a positive experience, we now had to face the ordeal of the appeals lodged by the thugs who killed Garry, which were due to be heard at the High Court later that month. As expected, two of them had appealed almost immediately, with both Swellings and Sorton using the procedure to claim their sentences were too harsh. I'm sure it would have been very convenient for them and their families not to have seen me there, but I was determined to go. As it turned out, Sorton didn't attend, but Swellings was there and, by the look of him, he appeared to have as little remorse as he did on the day he was sent to prison. There was the usual shifting of the blame; Swellings claimed he didn't know Garry could die as a result of the attack, and that it was Sorton, not him, who delivered the fatal kick. His barrister also said that Swellings just 'lit the blue touch paper' by hitting Garry, then stepped back for others to take over. It was the usual sickening pack of lies and attempts to wriggle out of a situation, the kind of thing that victims' families endure on a regular basis during such appeals. Fortunately, Lord Justice Moore-Bick and two other judges saw no reason to grant his appeal and upheld the original seventeen-year minimum term, as well as rejecting his appeal against the conviction itself. I was delighted by that, but less so that Sorton had his minimum sentence reduced by two years, taking it from fifteen to thirteen years before he can be considered for parole. It was decided that his age wasn't sufficiently taken into consideration at the time of sentencing. Lord Justice Moore-Bick did say, however, that, even when Sorton had served that term, he will not be released until the parole board is satisfied he no longer represents a danger to the public. I can only wish that 'the public' will include the Newlove family, who will never feel safe once he is out.

Afterwards, I was asked what I thought. 'We've lost Garry for the rest of our lives,' I said. 'We are on a life sentence and

I just hope and pray that the criminal justice system will stop wasting public money on appeals and think of the victims' families who need help to get through every day. I am going to fight so that victims' families don't have to suffer like we have.'

I had to pay my own train fare, and that of the girls, down to London for those appeals. Unlike Swellings, Sorton and, later, Cunliffe, there was no £500,000 of taxpayers' money in the form of legal aid to assist me. Since Garry's death, I've met countless victims' families who all say the same thing – that the justice system and appeals procedure is weighted heavily in favour of the defendants and against the victims and their families. Time after time, these poor people are forced to wait for months while lawyers pore over the cases of criminals who have ruined their lives, and then have to sit in court where they are treated as second-class citizens. I was able to have my say about Swellings' and Sorton's appeals, but only to the press outside court, and only because our situation is a high-profile one. There are thousands more victims' families out there who don't have such a voice, and who are overlooked and under-informed year after year after year. In short, it stinks, and that is why I continue to campaign for all those people who, like me, have become victims of crime through no fault of their own and find out they have little say in what happens in court.

As a family, we got through another Christmas – never an easy time for anyone bereaved – and in January I took the girls away to Egypt. My birthday is on 28 December and I'm not keen on New Year at the best of times, so it was a good moment to get away from it all. We had a much better time than we did in Barbados, that's for sure.

I'd left my phone at home during our week's holiday and when I got back I'd missed a few calls from Natalie, one of the administrators at the Warrington Wolves Foundation. She told me she'd been asked to get involved with some filming for a new show hosted by Noel Edmonds. She asked if we would take part and invited me and the girls to London to watch the show being aired live. So the camera crew came up for the day and we didn't think anything more of it. Natalie sold our invitation to London as a bit of a girly weekend, with a visit to the studio included, so I said 'yes'. The programme was called *Noel's HQ* and was due to be broadcast on Sky One. And that's as much as I knew about it.

When we got there, we discovered the studio was the same one used for *The X-Factor* and we were all excited in case we spotted Simon Cowell wandering around. We didn't, but I was surprised when one of the producers asked if I could be mic'd up, as Noel himself might want to ask me a few questions. Of course I didn't mind – anything to help the Warrington Wolves Foundation – so they clipped a mic on to me and the girls, and we were first led out on to the studio floor and then on to a sofa. I now knew that this programme was about helping local campaigners and good causes, so, when Noel came on to the set and asked me about the Foundation, I was more than happy to say how good it was, and how it had helped us.

Then he started asking me about our campaign. When they screened the clip, they had edited it so that it was about our work alongside Warrington Wolves. I cringed when people started talking about me being an inspiration and really wanted to get off the set. Noel then said that it was actually me and the girls who were being honoured. The girls began to cry as Noel told us that we would be getting our own radio frequency, equipment and training. I just didn't know what to say, or how to thank him. I also didn't know how to tell him that we'd just bought the equipment ourselves!

To add to the surprise, the radio DJ Neil Fox came out of the wings to tell us that he and his fellow DJs from the Bauer Media Group would support Newlove FM, including giving us their time as guest presenters when the station was up and running.

'You are a real inspiration,' he said to us as we sat there, mouths hanging open. 'As soon as we heard from *Noel's HQ* about your plans to bring music and opportunity to the community, we all wanted to be involved and are looking forward to helping you set up and promote the station.'

Unfortunately, it was difficult to concentrate on what he was saying because, by this time, I had lost it and was blubbering like a baby. If anyone thinks that these types of shows are staged, believe me they should just watch the four of us bawling our eyes out.

Well, that was brilliant news and it took the idea of a community radio station to a whole new level. Even though we'd already bought the equipment, which was portable enough to take into schools or lend out to community groups, having the backing of Noel Edmonds and Neil Fox, among others, meant that the publicity we got would enable the Newlove Warrington project to run further than we might otherwise have expected. Bauer's help also meant we were able to get the licence application through quickly. They also promised to help us with the installation of the aerial on the roof of the rugby club when the time came to do that, and the training would really help our Zoe, who was determined to be one of the station's main presenters.

One of the next steps was to find some premises. I wanted these to be as central as possible, because the whole idea was to engage young people and I didn't want them to have to catch buses or get lifts to some out-of-the-way place on an industrial estate. Somewhere in Warrington town centre would be perfect, so we were delighted when we were offered the use of an empty shop in Golden Square. The station would last two weeks, and in that short time we hoped to make a big impact on Warrington by demonstrating that local young people were a decent bunch, and that we would all work together to make the town better for every resident. It would be the country's first 'pop-up' radio station. I was thrilled when the shopping centre manager Ian Cox got involved and he couldn't have been kinder. For the next year, I really felt it gave us a prominent position so that people would recognise what we were doing.

In the weeks running up to the launch, which was scheduled for 27 June 2009, we appealed for volunteers to help man the station through 336 hours of continual broadcasting. Of this, we wanted 80 per cent chat and 20 per cent music, so there was a lot of time to fill. We had tremendous guidance and fantastic support from Chester University Radio Department, who were outstanding. Without their help, I honestly think we would have struggled. Zoe was to be one of the breakfast-show presenters, along with Vicky Duncalf and Vic McGlynn, and I thought the 7 a.m. start would be the perfect excuse to drag her out of bed!

Now we were beginning to book guests for interview slots, including players from Warrington Wolves who would take part in a special sports show, as well as other celebrity guests including politicians. And not just any politicians, either . . .

FIFTEEN

Making a Difference

Not long after the end of the trial, I had received a long email which congratulated me on my statement and claimed to support a lot of what I'd said. It was a very articulate and thoughtful email, and it promised to help me in any way. It was signed 'David Cameron'.

'Yeah,' I thought, 'and I'm the Queen.'

I rang Cheshire Police and told them I'd got an email from someone claiming to be the Leader of the Opposition and, while I thought it was well written, I considered it to be fake. They asked me to forward it over. A few hours later, they came back to me. It was genuine, sent from David Cameron's private address.

Being a polite person, I emailed back, thanking him for his comments and telling him that I wasn't sure if it was a genuine email or not. I said I welcomed his offer of help, and that it would be nice if we could meet up (although I appreciated he was busy).

Well, I didn't hear anything back from that. I waited a week or so then I got in touch again, this time rather more caustically. 'Politicians,' I said, 'you're all the same! Promises, promises.'

Almost immediately, I had a reply. He'd been on holiday, he

said, 'But that was no excuse.' He said he would like to meet me, and he put forward some tentative dates for a meeting in his office. I agreed, though I wasn't sure what we'd be talking about or whether he could genuinely help.

Anyway, we fixed a date and I went down to London. I have always been a Conservative voter, but I've never been very political. Like most people, I just want what I feel is right for my family and for society in general. So meeting the Conservative leader wasn't a big deal in the sense that I was in awe of the person who ran the party I support. I just wanted to meet someone of any political persuasion who would genuinely listen and was able to help. And David genuinely listened that day. We hit it off immediately and I found him to be a real 'people person'.

'Now,' you might say, 'she would say that,' but I tell it like it is and if I hadn't got on with him I'd have said so. But I felt he was genuinely interested in what I was trying to do. I was also keen to discuss his ideas about 'Broken Britain', the big Conservative campaign of that time, and how it chimed with my experience. If ever he needed a concrete example of Broken Britain, he only had to look at what happened to Garry. 'You're better educated than me,' I told him, 'and you're far wealthier, but we're all just people. You are in a powerful position and you need to do what you say you will do. Make sure you do what it says on the tin.'

I didn't preach, I just told him how it was in my world, and the worlds of millions of others affected by anti-social behaviour to any degree. I didn't expect anything from him – I was just glad to have the opportunity to offer up a 'true-life' story that might help shape his views. He didn't ask me who I voted for and I didn't tell him. To me, that was irrelevant. I always say I haven't the slightest interest if you are black, yellow, white or pink or what party you come from; we all have to work together to make our lives better and to make a difference in this world.

Getting Newlove Warrington off the ground and making real changes around the town was my sole aim. I had no agenda for a bigger platform, political or otherwise. To be honest, it was a big enough job looking after my family and working in Warrington.

I felt that we parted as friends – it certainly felt that way to me, anyway – and he said if he could help me he would. I met him on a couple of occasions after that, so when we were on the run-up to the launch of Newlove FM I thought it would be great to have him on as a special guest, talking about his ideas to tackle anti-social behaviour. I asked through his office and he agreed not only to back the station but also to give an interview with me and Nicksy, one of the professional DJs volunteering for us, from Capital Radio in London. He would be one of our first guests.

David Cameron is often portrayed as being protected from the real world by his birth, his background and his wealth. But I feel he is a man who has suffered greatly. Sadly, he lost his first child shortly before his beloved father died. His father had had both legs amputated. Life experiences like this, as I well know, change you forever as a human being. I found David to be far more empathetic and caring than a lot of people. It is extraordinary how some perceptions are overturned when you meet the living person. I have been disappointed when I have met others who have a stage persona but in real life are shallow and have wanted to use me. I've never felt that way about David.

So, celebrity guests and prominent politicians secured, we launched Newlove FM with one of Garry's favourite songs, 'In the Air Tonight' by Phil Collins. And from that moment on, until our two weeks was up, we had an absolute ball. The launch party was held in an Italian restaurant in Warrington where a few actors from *Hollyoaks*, *Emmerdale* and *Shameless* joined us. Our first news report was about the death of Michael Jackson – what a huge story to start with!

I did the interview as arranged with David Cameron, who spoke very eloquently on the subject of anti-social behaviour and justice for victims. However, he wasn't the only high-profile politician to speak to us. I'd put in a request to then Prime Minister Gordon Brown's office for an interview and, although his diary was booked up for months ahead, his secretary said a window would be found for us.

I was chuffed. Gordon Brown had been supportive and had written to me after Garry's death to express his sympathy. His handwriting was appalling – something he was later taken to task over in the press after he misspelled the name of a dead serviceman – but the sentiment was genuine. I now know it's because he is blind in one eye. It seems to me quite cruel when people who are household names are attacked by the media without the writer knowing the full facts. Gordon pre-recorded a 'down the line' interview with us to go out the following day, and then actually came on live because he was in Manchester. I rushed down there to grab the interview with him and he praised what we were doing as a 'very positive response to an appalling tragedy'. He was deeply concerned about the issues we were raising and, in fact, his advisers had to put a halt to the interview because he was running late and had a train to catch. I liked Gordon Brown. He was a genuinely nice person in a very tough job – one that perhaps didn't suit his personality. I guess you have to be careful what you wish for sometimes. He was kind enough to give me a signed copy of his book, and I was genuinely touched on the day of my ennoblement when Sarah Brown, his wife, came over to wish me well from both of them. It was a lovely gesture and I was very pleased.

Having the station in a shop was great, because it meant people could walk in off the street, see the DJs at work and get involved if they wanted to. And they did want to. There is some real talent out there, and it takes something like Newlove FM – or any other community effort, for that matter – to bring it out. We had two young lads come in one day; they were just ordinary boys but when they got on air they were as funny as Ant and Dec. We got them back in to do a little show on Warrington Walking Day and they were brilliant. (Warrington Walking Day is an annual event where all the faith schools parade in the town centre. It is heart-warming to see all the children in their best white dresses celebrating their schools.)

All in all, it was an excellent fortnight and we were very sad when the final show came to an end. Zoe especially loved the involvement and the experience she'd had, and I hadn't seen her so happy for a long time. As the eldest, she took on too much worrying about me and her sisters. It was great to see her young and carefree, and smiling and laughing again. The positive feedback we got from local people who'd either heard the station or been involved with it made the whole exercise very worthwhile.

A few months later, we were invited to a Bauer Media awards ceremony, at which Newlove FM scooped the prize for the best community station. I was overwhelmed, especially when Neil Fox came on and gave a lovely speech about us, and why he'd decided to get involved with Newlove FM.

It wasn't the only award we received that year. I had been put up for 'Cheshire Woman of the Year 2009', one of sixty women around the county nominated. I went to a ceremony at Eaton Hall with all these high-powered business and charity people and, to my shock, discovered I was the winner. I felt very emotional, particularly after one of the guests there that day told me she lit candles and said prayers for me. I was very humbled by that, and I said so in the speech I gave. I took home an engraved silver salver, which my mum now has.

Once all the excitement of the radio station was over, it was back to the day-to-day work of Newlove Warrington. We didn't have much money left and we were down to a staff of one (me), so I was using my savings to keep it going. I was keen to start the schools programme again so I toured local secondary schools, particularly in the run-up to Christmas, to warn about the dangers of under-age, uncontrolled and binge drinking. I also went into a few primary schools where I felt I should tone down the message somewhat. I found myself talking to nine and ten year olds who wondered how many units there were in a glass of whisky. That was an eye-opener, as were the secondary schools. I'd go along and join a kind of 'market place', where various agencies and organisations such as the police would gather at stalls in the school hall, talking to kids who wandered in. I lost count of the number of teenagers coming in looking tired and pale with bloodshot eyes, like they'd been at the sauce the night before and were still hungover. In my day, people would occasionally turn up to work looking like that, but never to school. I found it hard to understand parents who could allow their school-age kids to go out and get drunk. It was disheartening, but I was determined to keep spreading the message about excessive drinking and the catastrophic effects it can have on the individual and society. Kids would go very quiet when I told them, quite bluntly, about Garry's death and what it meant for us as a family. Was it making a difference? I hoped so, but you could never be sure.

I was also speaking a lot on behalf of victims' families, and the nightmare of the judicial process they had to go through during trials and appeals procedures. I knew about the horror of a trial, of course, and by now I was also experienced in the ways of the appeals system.

On a more local level, I was still pushing for something to be done about better facilities for Warrington's young people. I'd been talking to the town's council leaders but it felt like I'd have to move mountains to get anything done. It was very frustrating, particularly when I'd seen a brilliant example of what could happen in Warrington if only the will was there.

One evening, I was invited along to Bolton Lads & Girls Club, and I took the opportunity to have a look round at the facilities and to see if there was anything we could replicate in Warrington. The club was started in 1889 by local businessmen who wanted to do something to make the lives of boys working in the mills a bit happier. It is now the UK's biggest youth centre and thousands upon thousands of young people have enjoyed all it has to offer over the years. Membership was only £5 a year when I visited, and kids paid just 50p to get in. For that, the kids get access to a whole range of physical activities, plus arts and crafts, computer training and even a hot meal if they want. It's open seven days a week, fifty-one weeks of the year and it's just about the best youth facility I'd ever seen. The impact on the lives of the children it supports, and has supported in the past, is enormous.

To say I was blown away by the Lads & Girls Club is an understatement and I was sure it could be replicated in Warrington. Through Simon Moran, I met Nick Hopkinson, one of the club's directors, and he agreed to help me put the case for something similar. At the time of writing, the campaign is still on-going, but the economic downturn and cutting of youth facilities by councils right across the country has put any major plans on hold. But a youth café has now been set up for Warrington, which is a start, and Nick has been working with Warrington Youth Club to attract more members. I'm very grateful for what has been done so far and I hope that when the economy returns to better health the funding will be found for a 21st-century youth facility that meets the needs of all the town's youngsters. Or maybe some philanthropist or lottery winner will step forward with a cheque!

Around this time, I started to have a serious think about what I'd do next. Now I'd started campaigning against anti-social behaviour and for the rights of victims' families, I felt I couldn't just stop, but funding was a problem. The recession had really started to bite by then and I wondered how generous people could be when they themselves were feeling the pinch. The simple fact was that I needed a job. The thought of working as a legal PA again, dealing with issues that, while important to those involved, seemed trivial compared to my own experiences, was one I didn't relish, but I knew I had to do something, and that was the work I was trained for. My savings were almost gone and the girls were still at home. If I was to carry on campaigning, it would have to be in my spare time.

It's strange how often fate intervenes when you have a big decision to make, and a phone call was about to take me in a totally unexpected direction.

SIXTEEN

An Unexpected Honour

I was still mulling over all the various issues related to going back to work – and wondering whether anyone would actually employ me again, given that I'd been all over the newspapers for the previous two years – when I came home one Saturday afternoon to discover there was a message on my landline.

'Hi, Helen,' said the voice, 'it's David Cameron here. Sorry to have missed you. There's something I'd like to discuss with you, if you have a moment. Never mind, I'll try to call you this evening. Bye for now.'

Now, it wasn't entirely out of the blue to get a phone call from David. He was good at keeping in touch, particularly as we'd carried out a few speaking engagements together. In fact, I'd just spoken at the 2009 Conservative Party conference, telling a fringe debate that there should be more support for the victims of crime to get the compensation they deserve. So, when he rang back that evening, I expected that he'd be asking me to do it again at another event.

'No, it's not that I was ringing about,' he said, 'though I hope you will continue to speak out. I want to discuss something with you. I've been thinking that you would be an ideal person to take a seat on the benches in the House of Lords.

'I think you'd be a great advocate in the House for victims of crime and you've proved to be a very powerful lady,' he added. 'We need people from all backgrounds in the Lords and you're a real person. So many people can relate to you.'

David told me he couldn't make the final decision, but he was keen to put me forward if I was interested.

'Don't give me your answer yet,' he said. 'Put the phone down and think about it very carefully. When you're ready, call me back. The only thing I'd ask is that, if you want to go for it, you don't mention it to anyone until it's happened.'

'Of course,' I said, wondering how I'd keep such a massive secret to myself for the best part of a year.

I put down the phone and sat on the chair for a long time. The House of Lords? What did I know about that place? Wasn't it full of posh people who made the rules for the rest of us to follow? How would I fit in there? I only ever paid attention to what happened in the Commons. And was it a job he was offering me? If it was, how could I afford to live in London? So many questions . . .

Sorry, David, but I broke my promise to you that evening. When I'd come round from the shock, I spoke to my mum and, swearing her to secrecy, told her about the phone conversation I'd just had.

'Oh my God!' she said. 'I can't believe it! Do you realise what an honour it is to be asked?'

To be honest, that side of it hadn't really sunk in yet but judging by my mum's response it was a hell of a big deal.

'What are you going to do?' she asked.

'I really don't know, Mum. I'm not sure if it's a job or a title or what. And what do I do about the girls? I can't just clear off to London and leave them, can I? And where will I live?'

'The girls will be fine,' she said. 'They're on their own paths now and they've got each other, and me and your dad. They'll be fine, and they'll be proud of you. Do it for them.'

I needed to know more about what becoming a member of the Lords entailed, so I did what everybody else in the world does and Googled it. It seemed that there would be allowances attached to the role, which could provide some kind of income. It would be a squeeze, but I could do it. I'd been managing on very little for a while now and I was used to it. I never touched a penny of Newlove Warrington money, and even paid for my own travel. The only other people I needed to sound out to see if this could work were the girls. If they vetoed it, that was the end of that. I couldn't and wouldn't leave them without their full blessing. So it was an anxious time of waiting until I could tell them about it.

I broached the subject in a roundabout way: how would they feel if I was offered a job living away from home for part of the week. Would they be able to manage without me?

'Mum, go for it!' they chorused, when I sat them down for a family conference. 'Don't worry about us, we'll be fine.'

Well, they would say that, being three teenagers. But I knew I could trust them. After everything they'd been through, they were as close as they could be, and very sensible. They didn't seem to be bothered about my working away from home. As they said, they had plenty of family support. I was concerned about being able to look after them financially though. Houses with teenage girls incur enormous expenses, not least electricity bills, and I wasn't convinced I could manage. Still, I'd been offered an opportunity to carry on my campaigning work at the heart of government, and I'd be a fool to turn that down over the excessive use of hairdryers. A few days after our initial conversation, I phoned David Cameron and told him it would be an honour to accept his offer.

'That's great news, Helen,' he said, sounding very pleased.

'I'll put the wheels in motion as far as putting you forward is concerned, and I'll ask Lord Strathclyde to give you a call and run over a few things with you. OK?'

'OK,' I said, wondering who this grand-sounding man was.

I needn't have worried. When he called, the then Leader of the Opposition in the Lords couldn't have been more charming and friendly. He asked me various questions, including whether I'd ever donated to the Conservative Party. I was not too sure what he meant, but he explained that if I had given them a million pounds – as you do! – it would call into question whether I had bought my peerage.

'Donated?' I said. 'My girls go through more money than the Conservative Party – I haven't got the funds to donate!'

Lord Strathclyde explained that, once my residency and nationality was approved, I'd have to put together a CV that would go up to the then Prime Minister, Gordon Brown, for his approval. 'Well, that'll be one side of A4 then,' I said, laughing.

'Don't worry,' Lord Strathclyde said. 'There are ways of doing these things and David's office will help you draft it.'

And so began several months of waiting and wondering what might happen next. After Christmas 2009, General Election talk was in the air and nothing could happen to my application until that had been dealt with and the winner announced. Fortune seemed to favour the Tories – the country was well in recession by then and, after 13 years in power, Labour seemed to be taking most of the blame for it – and it looked and felt like David Cameron could be the next Prime Minister. If so, it was likely I'd be setting foot through the door of the Lords for the first time, along with all the other newly elevated peers. Of course, David didn't need to become PM before I could be given a peerage. All the party leaders select their own candidates then pass their nominations on to the current PM before the Queen gives the final approval.

However, until the election was finalised, and my appointment was confirmed – or not – there was nothing I could do about finding a job. It was a worrying time and I had to keep everything quiet.

In the meantime, I carried on campaigning and raising awareness around victims' rights, anti-social behaviour and young people and alcohol. The more I learned about binge drinking and its effects in the community, the more I realised what a huge issue it had become, not just in Warrington but right across the country. Much of what I discovered genuinely shocked me. As I've mentioned, during the making of the *Dispatches* programme, I went round the country trying to get answers to the various problems to which our family had fallen victim. One of these visits was to Rhyl, in North Wales, where the police were having a very hard time controlling anti-social behaviour caused by binge drinking. Shopkeepers had resorted to using 'mosquito' devices – little electronic gadgets that emitted a high-pitched sound – outside premises where kids congregated. This moved them on, but only to other areas where they would cause trouble. The police carried with them all sorts of equipment, including urine-testing sticks which could be slotted into a hand-held portable device. They also had cameras, which would record abusive behaviour that could be used in evidence. We followed the police to a park, where they came across a group of youths sprawled across the grass, drinking from large bottles of Coke. They weren't being abusive but they did get defensive when they were asked if what they were necking back was purely soft drink.

'All right,' said one of them, 'there's just a little bit of whisky in there, that's all.'

The WPC tested his bottle on the spot and it was absolutely full of the stuff, enough to blow your head off. The officers emptied the bottles, but they weren't convinced it would stop them drinking again that day. Their suspicions proved correct later on, when we came across another group of lads drinking cans of Stella on a wall. The beer was taken off them, but a few hours later they were caught again – obviously, they'd simply managed to get hold of some more.

I found it hard to believe that young people could be so dependent on booze in order to have a good time and would go to any lengths to get it. Even my own kids thought I was being naive. 'Mum, you'll not stop it,' they said. 'It's the parents. They let their kids drink at home, and when they've had enough they just drop them off somewhere so it's not happening round their way.'

This was a revelation to me. I've been lucky that I haven't had alcohol-related problems with my children – most likely because of what happened to their father – but as they've grown up they've told me they know that parents freely allow their kids to get bladdered. In fact, I've even had parents ask me, 'How much drink is Amy allowed?' and I say, 'She's not allowed any – she's 16!' To my mind, even supplying them with a bit of alcohol is encouraging them; it gives them the green light to think, 'It's OK, Mum and Dad don't mind if I get wasted.' The number of times I've heard of teenage parties ending up in fights, damage, noise and anti-social behaviour, and it's usually because parents either don't know or don't care that their kids are out drinking. Or maybe they want to be 'friends' with their kids instead of parents, or they have fallen into the trap of succumbing to 'pester power'. This starts when they are younger, whining about sweets at the supermarket checkout, and continues when they are older about alcohol.

And yet most of us have been silly about alcohol at least once as youngsters. Alcohol hasn't just been invented. Young people have always experimented with drink, overdone it and regretted it the following day (or not, as the case may be). What seems to be different now is peer pressure to drink as much as possible, as young as possible, and seemingly with the tacit approval of parents. The parents of my generation would never have allowed their kids to get drunk at home before turfing them out in search of trouble. Today, parents are put under pressure by other parents whose kids are allowed to drink, and if alcohol is freely available at other people's houses it is very difficult for those parents who don't condone under-age drinking to say 'no'. How would those pro-drinking parents feel if the situation was different, and we weren't talking about drink, but heroin? Naturally, they would be horrified and scared. So why do they think drinking is a safe option for their offspring? It can kill them or, as we know only too well, they can kill others under its influence. Excessive drinking can lead to long-term health problems, psychological damage and sometimes a criminal record. Getting so drunk that you can't stand isn't clever or cool, yet by turning a blind eye parents are saying a tacit 'yes' to under-age drinking.

Losing a loved one is the biggest reality check anyone can ever have and, while I'd never wish my experience on another person, as far as young people and alcohol are concerned, we all need that reminder. We are not powerless; there is so much we could do as individuals but we are up against a rising problem that, year on year, seems to be growing. As a nation, we don't seem to have a brake on our drinking, like so many Europeans do. They drink lightly, over meals and in the early evening with friends, and they know when to take a break and when to stop altogether. In the UK, some people just carry on for as long as they can before they're sick, or become unconscious or get arrested. No wonder the age at which liver problems are detected is becoming younger and younger.

I'm not a party pooper; I enjoy a drink out as part of a meal with friends but we have to start encouraging everyone to adopt social drinking if they are of age and stamp out for good the anti-social drinking that makes us a laughing stock in the eyes of more disciplined nations.

We're doing a good job of educating people about the dangers of smoking, and decisive action has been taken in terms of cigarette advertising and strict controls on their sale. So why can't we do the same with alcohol? I think we need to be more graphic, to be honest; the recent adverts that showed a young person's night out in reverse, with them looking a terrible drunken mess at the beginning, were clever but they didn't have much impact on me. How about showing exactly what a diseased liver looks like, much the same as lungs affected by smoking-related cancer? However, even that might not make much difference. Boozing seems to be sanctioned as a worthwhile, even honourable, activity, and few young people see anything wrong with getting completely wrecked at the weekend. Supermarkets have a place in promoting responsible drinking that includes marketing and display. If you shop at Costco and you want to buy cigarettes, you pay for them first and collect them from another area. That's a good idea because the shop assistant handing them out can see the person coming to collect them, and whether they're old enough to have them. It's a system that could work with alcohol; at the moment, everything going through one checkout, with a long queue of people behind and a tired and harassed shop worker at the till, is far from ideal.

I've been accused of stigmatising young people in relation to alcohol consumption, but I don't mean to. Under-age drinking is illegal for a reason. It damages a growing body's health. It removes inhibitions and makes a person vulnerable. It can also exacerbate bad behaviour. We shouldn't encourage street drinking either. Excessive drinking wrecks lives; it wrecked mine, and those of my girls, and while we are trying to piece our lives back together they will never be the same. It also wrecks the lives of the drinker's family in that they have to deal with drunkenness, violence and, in some cases, prison.

I find it sad to see just how many local pubs are shutting down. The pub was once the hub of the community and one of the few places you could buy alcohol. Any misbehaviour in a local pub was swiftly dealt with, the offender was barred and the whole community knew about it. It was a rite of passage for an 18 year old to be taken in by his dad for his first drink, and that was no bad thing. It taught youngsters how to drink responsibly, and not show themselves up in public. Nowadays, that's vanishing, and the prevailing wisdom is to head to one of the many '2-for-1', or 'ladies free all night' places and drink yourself stupid. It seems that, to enjoy yourself, you have to be drunk. In a world that claims to be closely connected, via internet, email and mobile, I think that says a lot about what society has become. It's very sad. People say I'm old and, yes, I probably do sound like my mother, but I don't care and I make no apologies for it. If I can change even one young person's mind about alcohol, and prevent them from going out, getting absolutely paralytic and ruining their lives or those of other people, I'll have done my job.

SEVENTEEN

The Baroness Newlove
of Warrington

Speaking on camera is something I never expected to do, at least before August 2007, and, while I still occasionally feel that I'm the wrong person to be fielding questions, the experience of being on telly has become a necessary part of the work I do and the goals I want to achieve. I am never comfortable being the centre of attention and having lots of eyes on me, as I am a very private person. I don't have any ego but I do what I do because I take the job I have been given seriously, speaking out for others like me.

I am fiercely protective of my daughters. Garry's murder pushed us into the limelight and there seems to be an insatiable interest in us. I am always asked if they will appear in youth or educational programmes or give quotes and I have refused. The memory of them having to give evidence at Chester Crown Court was more than enough for me to want to protect them from trial by media. However, when the producers from ITV's *Real Crime* approached me with a view to making a documentary about us, the girls were keen to be involved – and to speak frankly on camera about what happened on the night their dad was attacked.

I'd seen the programme before and knew it was well made and faithful to the story. They use a mixture of interviews, photos, footage and reconstruction with actors to shape the narrative without over-dramatising it. It's presented by Mark Austin, whom I've always found to be a very credible newsman.

After a long talk with the girls, we agreed to let the *Real Crime* researchers visit us and get the content together for the programme. Our story is well known, of course, but this would be the first – and possibly last – time the girls would speak publicly about the events. They were nervous, of course, but they felt strong enough now to tell it as they saw it. They were there, and it was only right that an in-depth programme like *Real Crime* should feature them. I believe it couldn't have been made without their help.

Zoe was interviewed alone; Danielle and Amy together. I had no influence over what they said, and wouldn't have interfered anyway. As in court, they would relate the facts of what happened clearly and simply. I would give my own account of events, as would the police. Representing the press was *News of the World* reporter Keith Gladdis, a journalist I knew and trusted. He would sum up the public's reaction to what happened and explain why it had such a big impact. The production team also interviewed Howard and Christine Malone, who had been our neighbours in Station Road North. They talked about events in the run-up to the night Garry was attacked and how trouble had been brewing for a while.

When the programme came out, in the summer of 2010, we were reassured by its sincerity. The production team had done an excellent job. The dramatisation of the events and the courtroom scenes were very accurate, and the three youths who played Swellings, Sorton and Cunliffe, laughing, yawning and rolling their eyes in the dock, sent shivers up my spine. The only inaccuracy was that, in the reconstruction, it showed three people attacking Garry when actually there were more around him, fifteen or more at one point. They were all aged between 15 and 18, and girls were also present. But, for me, watching Zoe, Danielle and Amy took my breath away. They spoke plainly, but with heartbreaking honesty and emotion, making it very difficult to watch. I had to put a cushion over my face as the tears welled up. These are my babies – the actions they saw and all the pain they have been through and still go through on a daily basis just makes me feel sick inside.

'How could anyone do that to someone?' Danielle said. 'I couldn't believe it was my dad lying there, covered in blood. The paramedics did everything they could to save him. I was just standing there, watching them work, and eventually they shut the ambulance doors so we couldn't see what they were doing.'

Zoe recalled, 'When I got to hospital and saw Dad I was just paralysed. I couldn't move. Danielle and Amy were talking to him, trying to get through to him, but I was rooted to the spot. I couldn't say goodbye, couldn't do anything at all.'

Amy said, 'As my dad went to confront the gang, I put out my hand and tried to grab him, to pull him back. I had a horrible feeling in my stomach that something was going to happen . . .'

'When I think about Amy, I start to cry,' Zoe admitted. 'Dad was a big part of her, like a big brother and a best friend. She says it's lonely without him, even though she has us.'

'Zoe and Danielle are like Dad, so he's not gone fully. I'm like him in a lot of ways – I do the things he would do,' Amy added. 'It's the quality of time with him that I miss.'

They all cried on camera, and so did I. Plenty more tears were spilled during the broadcast too. Afterwards, I felt the girls had given all that they could give. They need never talk to anyone else about that night and, so far, they never have. We all drove back home and I said to the girls, 'That is it now. We are all physically and emotionally drained – no more.'

As the spring of 2010 approached, thoughts turned to the General Election, which was now set for May. In the run-up to polling day, I'd done some campaigning work with David and Samantha Cameron in the north-west, taking them to Bolton Lads & Girls Club, and, while we seemed to be heading for a change of government, nothing was certain. As we now know, there was a hung Parliament and the Conservatives and Lib-Dems formed a coalition government. The Coalition said it would create a number of new peerages to balance the House of Lords according to shares of the vote won in the election. And yet I still hadn't heard whether I was going to be one. So imagine my surprise, on 24 May, when the lead story on the 'breaking news' ticker-tape running on *Sky News* was that: 'Widow of Garry Newlove is to be made a peer'. I was in my kitchen and just stared at the monitor wondering how it had come out, especially without my knowing first, but there it was.

Seconds after it appeared on Sky, my phone started ringing madly. My family and all the papers wanted to know if it was true, and how I felt. I had to say 'no comment' until I'd spoken to Number 10. I phoned David's office and spoke to a secretary, but even he didn't know as the decision had not been confirmed with them.

Anyway, the following day's papers all carried the story and, while I don't think I ever had it officially confirmed, it was obviously going ahead. At last, I could start telling my friends. They were so pleased, despite all the jokes about having to curtsey to me now!

My dear friend Rani was ecstatic when she heard about my peerage. She has a brilliant working knowledge of government and charities, and the help she has given to me is utterly invaluable. If it hadn't been for Rani, I don't know how I would've coped those first few years adapting in London to my new life.

But I'm getting ahead of myself. After the news broke, I needed to know what to do next. You don't get a job description when you enter the House of Lords, although I knew I'd be what's described as a 'working peer', and people from my background (which is most people) can't be expected to be familiar with all the pomp and circumstance involved. Luckily, there is one person inside the House who knows the place and its rituals inside out, and it was to him that I was dispatched a few weeks after my peerage was announced. Thomas Woodcock is the rather grandly titled Garter Principal King of Arms and he looks after new peers in terms of picking their title and, if they wish, a coat of arms.

A title? Me? The whole thing still seemed like it was a dream. As I wandered through the corridors of the House to meet Thomas, all I could think was that I'd somehow ended up at Hogwarts. That first impression didn't change much in the first few months either, as I struggled to get used to the 'old boy' rituals of the place. But I couldn't believe the respect and warmth I was shown by the staff. I still had to look around when they called me m'lady but their friendliness made me feel as if I really did belong there. Thomas was extremely helpful. I love history, and his knowledge of the House had me captivated.

As for my title, I couldn't be Baroness Newlove of Cheshire, as the area is geographically too big, so we had to narrow it down. I was born in Salford and had grown up in Irlam, but I'd started my family in Warrington, my parents lived there and, of course, it was where Garry died. So, after much deliberation, and I must say against the advice of some of my closest friends who worried about the connection, I chose Warrington. It is where my family live and where I have close connections. The Baroness Newlove of Warrington in the County of Cheshire would be my full title, and I was happy with that. The girls were very chuffed with that too, because there had never been a Newlove peer. I was *The* Baroness Newlove not 'the'. Overnight, of course, the girls all became honourables. I could've picked a crest but getting that together would've cost thousands and I don't have that kind of money. If I did, it would have been a great honour to have one. And to pass it on to my children and grandchildren. So, one day, who knows?

Once the title was chosen, Thomas sent off my 'letters patent' (in effect, my application for membership of the Lords) to the Queen, who, by signing it, agrees to the peerage being applied for. Eventually, these beautiful scrolls signed by Her Majesty arrived in a lined wooden casket with her seal inside. It was one of the proudest moments of my life to see my poor mum and dad gaze on it with tears in their eyes. As they both suffer from ill health, they have never been able to come to London to see me in the House of Lords, although my mother watches the live broadcasts daily.

Once that was done, things moved fairly quickly, and a date was arranged for a full induction day at the Lords so that all the new peers had some idea of what was ahead on the day of our ennoblement, and in the weeks and months after that.

My induction day was in June, and I'd never felt so intimidated in my life. It was also a very emotional day as it would have been my 24th wedding anniversary. Everyone else seemed so posh and appeared at ease with these grand surroundings. They included the former children's TV presenter Floella Benjamin and Shireen Ritchie – Guy Ritchie's stepmother and a local government official of many years' standing. Shireen was a lovely, gracious woman and I was deeply saddened when she passed away from cancer recently. She would have made a significant contribution to the House, I am sure.

By contrast, I felt like Hilda Ogden! The only people who

seemed down-to-earth were the doorkeepers and police officers, and I spent a considerable amount of time talking to them (and still do). We were shown round the House, including the Chamber itself, and introduced to a baffling list of rules and regulations, including the Code of Conduct for Members. I didn't have any such interests, other than furthering the cause of justice for victims of crime and trying to sort out alcohol abuse, but I still had to sign the updated Code, just in case.

I felt like the new kid on the block, excited and bewildered in turn. We were shown a DVD of the ennoblement ceremony, with everyone in their finery, and the whole thing gave me butterflies. Suppose I tripped, or walked the wrong way, or cried, or (worse still) laughed? How would I know where to sit? As for actually speaking, where on earth would I begin, and when? What would I say? All these questions swirled around my mind as I watched the ceremony, unable to imagine myself in ermine-trimmed robes, behind Black Rod and the rest of the splendidly dressed procession.

The great day finally came on 15 July 2010. I needed two 'supporters' for the procession to the Woolsack, the seat on which the Lord Speaker sits, so I asked Lord Strathclyde, the Leader of the House of Lords, and Baroness Warsi, then Co-Chairman of the Conservative Party, whom I'd previously met and got on well with. Sayeeda Warsi comes from the North like me and gave me a lot of sound advice on how to survive. I was humbled that they both agreed immediately, saying they'd be honoured.

I invited my family down to watch the ceremony. I knew there would be a lot of interest in my ennoblement, and I wanted to please everybody. So I contacted Sky TV and negotiated a 'loop' interview which would be pre-recorded and shared with everyone. Although my phone was ringing off the hook all that morning, I didn't answer it. The deal was that I didn't give any other interviews and I didn't want all the palaver of posing for photographs that day. It was a very important moment for me and my family. I wanted time to reflect on Garry and I didn't want it turned it into a three-ringed circus. I've never seen myself as a celebrity and I didn't want people to think that my appointment to the Lords was a flash in the pan. I was there to campaign, and do a good job in the House. I also wanted to absorb the ceremony from the start, so I went in early to avoid the photographers!

There is a set procedure to the ceremony and it's actually over quite quickly. There is a lot of nodding and bowing, and making sure you walk the correct way into the Chamber and out again. Then you pledge your allegiance to the Queen and sign the papers. I was incredibly nervous, not least because I knew my family was in the public gallery and that the parliamentary cameras were on me, and when I become nervous I develop a runny nose. So that wasn't much fun to contend with as I waited to go on. I read out the oath with hardly a breath, signed, then, as protocol states, shook the Speaker's hand to be welcomed into the House. Immediately, the House erupted in the traditional cheer given to new members. That was it. I was in!

Although it was surreal, it was an incredibly proud moment for me. The family and Rani, who had agreed to help me in the House, were all in tears. We had a lovely lunch and after all the tension I could finally relax. As I said, after the ceremony, Sarah Brown, the now former Prime Minister's wife, came over to say 'hello'. I'd never met her before but she seemed very down-to-earth and friendly and it was a very kind thing to do.

Lunch over, we got ready to go home. I was told camera crews were still lurking outside three hours later. They'd been asking the staff when we were likely to come out. I sent the family out one way and came out with the girls and Rani from another door. I was called over by someone with a mic and, before Rani could pull me back, I went to say hello because my mum brought me up not to be rude. So they stole an interview, breaking the agreement. Luckily, Sky thought it was amusing that I was so horrified and forgave me.

I learned later that you can't get involved in the business of the House until you've made your maiden speech. While I had no intention of taking as long as Michael Heseltine (who famously waited 11 years before making his speech!), I didn't plan to just jump in either. I needed to absorb the place first, find my way around and get used to its workings. For that I needed a mentor and I was lucky enough to be assigned Trish Morris, otherwise known as Baroness Morris of Bolton. I couldn't have asked for someone kinder, wiser and more understanding. It helped that we're both from the north-west, so she understood where I was coming from and how I felt about joining 'the Establishment'. She's also involved with Bolton Lads & Girls Club, so we had similar views on cutting youth crime and providing better facilities for young people.

Trish's help was invaluable but I knew she was busy and I didn't want to bother her with every little question niggling me. I also believe the best way of learning something is to go and discover it for yourself, so one afternoon during that summer, when I knew the House was quiet, I went down to London and decided to just get on with it. I was determined to go into the Chamber alone, so I opened the great double doors that lead to the Chamber and walked in. I stared around at the red benches, looking for a familiar face. There wasn't one, so I headed for the right-hand side, knowing that was where the government benches were. I sat down and started to listen to whoever was speaking at the time, feeling quite pleased with myself.

After a few minutes, I began to feel something wasn't right.

Suddenly, I realised I was on the opposite side to where I'd sat for a short while after my ennoblement. Oh, God, I was on the Opposition benches! There were two sets of doors and I had gone in the wrong one. I sat frozen to the spot, not daring to get up and cross the floor in case I broke some protocol or other. I could feel myself starting to sweat and hoped the cameras hadn't spotted me. There was a little commotion and some whispering around me. And a lot of friendly smiles. Then, a Labour peer (thankfully, I've forgotten who) turned round from the bench in front and handed me a note.

'Dear Baroness Newlove,' it said, 'much as we'd love to have you sitting with us, we're sorry to tell you you're sitting on the wrong side. It is not compulsory but you might want to join your colleagues.'

I went crimson and looked around. Luckily, Rani was in the public gallery and she'd noticed what was going on. She summoned a doorkeeper, who crept into the Chamber and discreetly told me that I was on the wrong side.

'I know,' I said, 'but I'm too terrified to move. What do I do?'

'Don't worry,' he said, 'just get up now and follow me out. Then you can come back in – on the right side.'

He smiled broadly and I noticed a few stifled laughs and bitten lips around the House. I felt such a ninny, but as soon as I came out I had to laugh.

'Oh my God,' I said to the doorkeeper, 'what an idiot! That's what you'd call a Bridget Jones moment.'

'Don't worry,' he said. 'We all make mistakes. Mind you, it'll make a great little news item for the House of Lords newsletter.'

I wasn't allowed to forget it easily either. Later, my mentor Trish had heard we were on a three-line whip to vote, which is life or death. As I waited in the Peers Entrance to meet her, the division bells rang, meaning that a vote is taking place. I was panicking and thought, 'I need to get up to the Chamber to vote,' and so decided I couldn't wait for her any longer. I told Rani where I was going and followed my colleagues to the division lobby. Trish came rushing in and shouted over to Rani, 'Where is she? Has she voted?'

Rani said, 'Yes, and she's voted on the right side!'

I am sure they all thought I really needed a minder until I got used to the place. But thankfully the doorkeepers came to my rescue and steered me the right way. They are fantastic people. I met Trish coming out of the division lobby and she apologised for the delay and was thankful that I had managed to get to vote down the correct corridor.

There are countless rules and protocols, which are so daunting that you sometimes feel you will never suss this place out. But, although there was a lot to learn, because the summer was quiet I had some time to catch up. As the days went by and I got used to processes and procedures, I began to wonder whether every day would be like this. Little did I know that, by October, it would be a different ball game altogether, and far busier than I could ever have imagined.

As I would have to move to London sooner or later, I had to come to a decision about whether we kept the family home in Warrington. Since Garry's death, I'd been in the public eye, of course, but being ennobled took this to a whole new level and I didn't want the press camped at my door for a quote whenever something relevant came along, especially when I wasn't there and the girls were. That wasn't fair on them, so we had a long family discussion and it was decided that we would leave Warrington altogether.

It was not an easy decision to make. Amy wanted to stay because she felt her dad was still there in spirit, a feeling I fully understood and empathised with. My mum and dad were still living there too, and seeing them wouldn't be as easy or as frequent as it had been. Despite that, I knew I'd be worrying if I felt the girls were alone in Warrington, and they knew Mum had to concentrate and get on with the job. So we moved, and found a lovely place to rent while we looked around for something more permanent. For security reasons, I can't say where, but I've always loved the place and now when I come home at weekends I feel much healthier and happier than I did before.

I had no idea where I should live in London. Budget was all-important but I also didn't want to end up in a risky area. I didn't know the place at all (and I'm still getting used to it) and I had to be guided by others. Although I don't walk terribly well (the result of an operation on my foot that has left me with a limp), I tried to avoid the Tube whenever possible. I hate it – it feels so claustrophobic and tense, and I'm always worried about being recognised by some nutter down there, and no one coming to my aid. I find London so expensive – my hair nearly shot off when I went into a newsagent's one day and bought a can of Coke! – and it feels too fast paced and packed. Perhaps you get used to it in the end, but I'm always glad when the weekend comes and I can catch the train home to the family and oodles of fresh air.

I found a place in Pimlico. It sounds grand, but actually it wasn't – it was more like a flat-share, which is the reality for quite a number of peers, particularly those travelling from the North. Becoming a baroness does not make you rich, despite what many people think! Keeping a roof over my head, and over the kids' heads, plus all the other costs took a huge chunk out of my daily allowance. In addition, as a working peer, I needed to be close to the House in order to vote. It's not as if I could take a full-time job doing something completely different, and pop into the House now and again for tea.

David Cameron told me he wanted me to be a 'voice for

victims' in Parliament, but other than that I wasn't sure what I'd be doing. He wanted me to first absorb my surroundings, get used to the place and become involved slowly, taking small steps. It was the best advice I've ever had. I was inundated with letters, emails and phone calls. Many victims sent me such pitiful letters and, unfortunately, sometimes less than sincere individuals tried to get me to support their work. I could easily have made the fatal mistake of jumping into things too soon.

In October 2010, I was called to a meeting with David and the Home Secretary, Theresa May. He told me he was pleased with my progress in the Lords so far and that I'd got to grips with a lot of things in a short space of time. He felt that I wasn't intimidated by the world of politics and that I could do an enormous amount of good 'in the field'. To that end, he and Theresa said they were appointing me to the role of Government Champion for Active, Safer Communities. My work as a peer was about to begin in earnest.

EIGHTEEN

Championing Communities

My new role as Government Champion would involve quite a lot of travel. David explained that he wanted me to go out and talk to grassroots community activists, plus business people, police, youth workers and others, to find out what worked and what didn't in terms of creating safer communities. I would spend several months doing this, which would culminate in a report to Whitehall ministers advising how government and local agencies could empower such communities. I'd be looking at identifying a cluster of neighbourhoods as 'test-beds' for promoting stronger and more integrated community activism and my role was to break down barriers that existed to prevent such places working successfully together for a better future.

'Today we want to start inspiring people all round the country to get involved,' I said, when my appointment was announced, 'by showcasing the excellent work already done and freeing people to take part.

'The government is creating the right environment for community-level activity to flourish by giving local people power over policing priorities and ending top-down government.

'But for a real revolution to happen we need all the existing groups to help spread their success far and wide – if every group already doing good work now helps another, we will see a real cultural shift.'

I would have a team of people to work with at the Home Office and I remember when I was introduced to my staff and shown my office. I couldn't believe it was so big. As a PA, I'd always sat outside the boss's office and here I was now, with one of my own. It was hard to take in.

First, we had to establish which communities we would focus on, which had the 'activists' – local people who worked hard, often unpaid, to better their neighbourhoods – as well as where and what was the 'magic ingredient' that set them apart from others who were less successful. This was at a time when the nature of the Big Society was being hotly debated. David Cameron was convinced it was out there and we could find many examples of people already living the ideal. Cynics were dismissing it and, as the terrible state of the economy began to be revealed, not only was there no money – as famously mentioned by a departing Treasury Minister on a Post-it note for the new Coalition government – but there was also an IOU in the national till of billions of pounds!

I was adamant that we wouldn't waste time or resources on places that had already had some attention. I wanted real people and real examples. I was presented with a long-list of suitable communities that, I was told, had real potential. The policy team were set to do the groundwork and make sure we'd identified the right ones.

As my name was on this project, I wanted to lead it. I wanted a diverse range of communities with a good mixture of needs and resources, and we settled on seven we thought best represented what we were looking for. The areas picked were: Town and Park Wards, Merthyr Tydfil (South Wales); Offerton (Stockport); the Briar Road Estate in Havering; Cutsyke (Wakefield); Cheriton and Folkestone East (Shepway); the parish of St John's in Hackney; and the Flower Roads Estate in Southampton.

There were other areas but I needed to feel comfortable and be sure that they were the correct ones who needed extra assistance. I know I was an enigma – and probably a pain in the butt! – to policy officials who had to work with me. I'm not sure if they had come across anyone who would not roll over when pushed, or one who would not go quietly if things were not working out. I'm more likely to sit up and have my say. I'm no one's puppet and I have no wish or inclination to play silly buggers with anyone with a hidden agenda. I am who I am and am not prepared to compromise my values. I say to everyone: I am not a minister, I am not a politician or a civil servant. If I feel that they baffle me with their language, then how the hell do they expect the people on the ground to understand the message? What I do and say is based on the terrible experiences I have been through and I am passionate about representing others who may not be fortunate enough to have the ear of the high and mighty. I'll work my heart out alongside you, but only if you have the same ideals and dreams as me.

I am also aware that this opportunity may only be a short window. I am under no illusion that one day you can be flavour of the month but the next you can be fish and chip paper. But it is who you are inside that matters. There is an old proverb I quote when anyone ever asks for my help or profile to promote their cause: 'Beware of what you wish for – you just might get it.' I may be thought of as a 'loose cannon' by people who don't understand me, but what you see is what you get with me. I have many wonderful friends. I work alongside the police, top and bottom ranked. I am a judge on the Police Bravery Awards and feel very honoured to be there. I haven't got the time or patience for mind games especially when they affect people's lives. But I am a firm and loyal friend and defender of those whom I think have a good heart and a real ambition to make societal changes that will make this country a better place.

Back to my seven 'Newlove Neighbourhoods', as they were named by the press. They were each given £15,000 and told to use it in their communities to improve their lives. They are real people who are quietly making a real difference and I am overjoyed at their progress; we just needed to break down bureaucratic barriers, cut red tape and let them be free to find local solutions to their local problems.

The full stories of the efforts people were making to change their communities is a book in itself and I can't possibly do justice to all those stories here. What I can say is that I was both humbled and inspired by the dedication and determination they had to make their lives, and those of future generations, better, safer and more fulfilled. My idea was to bring these communities together via the creation of a network between some or all of them, which would facilitate the sharing of ideas and information. I wanted to do away with the supposed North/South divide and bring together examples of best practice, wherever it was found. It's amazing how caught up in London you can get. Working alongside academics, policy people and other professionals makes you realise how insular people become and they can tend to think that London is the only place to be. It makes me so frustrated. There are many examples of good practice outside of London too, which London could benefit from if only they'd listen occasionally. Personally, I like to pinch their good ideas and bring them back up North! It's amazing what we can do if we not only share data, resources and good practice but also move it geographically for all of us to reap the rewards.

I had six months to visit these seven neighbourhoods, listen to their experiences and gather information to use in my report. I wanted to work closely with those on the ground who knew their neighbourhoods best and, while it did indeed involve a lot of travelling, I knew that face-to-face contact would be invaluable. What I couldn't do was write a typical government report full of jargon and civil-service speak. I had no experience of that, and didn't want to communicate that way anyway. This was to be a report by an activist for activists, detailing in plain language what I'd found and how I thought changes could be made. I said in the introduction that this was to be a living report, not some dry government document with no life or substance to be filed on some dusty shelf. I wanted real people's voices to shout out to agencies and government.

One of my first trips out of London was to Cutsyke, in Wakefield. This was a 'deprived area' (a term I personally hate, along with 'affluent', as it tars everyone with the same brush), notorious for its drugs problem and high levels of crime. And yet there was a real community spirit on that estate, with people willing to help others. The centre of this community group was a downstairs flat on the estate's worst road, which they had rented, and they eventually expanded to rent the whole house. Here, the group had begged and borrowed some computers and set up a suite where kids could do their homework and older residents learn how to use modern technology. They also took over a plot of land and turned it into a garden, so that older people could show younger ones a thing or two about looking after and cultivating green space. Very subtly, the community, young and old, was beginning to work together and skills were being passed between the two groups. This gave the kids the idea that there was a point to learning from the older generation, and it broke down prejudices on the part of older people towards the younger ones.

Rheta Davison, MBE, was part of that community group. She said that young people always had something to offer; it was a case of finding it, and getting them to do something with their talents rather than sitting at home. In the report, Rheta offered some tips for setting up a group:

> My advice to other groups is be dogmatic. If you are passionate about your area then you will succeed but you have to keep punching away at bureaucratic jargon and the stigma of being a voluntary activist. Some workers will look down on you and try and make you trip up in many ways. But if you have to confront someone (a councillor or council officer) make sure you have all the relevant information with you so you can back up your argument.

There was a similar young/old divide in Havering. When I first arrived, we had an introductory meeting. The older people of the community sat to my left and the kids were on my right! The youngsters had made a DVD about the area, which highlighted how bad it had become, and one of their criticisms was that older people 'should go to bed early', presumably instead of complaining about the young people. During the debate I attended, the older ones fought back, accusing the kids of looking intimidating by having their hoods up all the time. I sat in the middle of all this, feeling like the referee! However, the youngsters told them that by saying they should be indoors by 8 p.m. they just meant that they were concerned for their safety. Wearing hoodies – because they were cold and wanted to keep warm – and huddling up in gangs did not always mean they were bad. They explained that if they were in a bigger group than the ones hanging around another corner, they simply felt they had safety in numbers and nothing more sinister. Perceptions are not always correct. Clearly, there was a lot to do to sort out this divide, but within a few weeks of that meeting, and with some suggestions of a way forward, things had really changed. A rap 'opera' involving young and old was written and performed, and a photography club was set up so that everyone could contribute their thoughts about the area in a visual way. The vibe when we met again was so different and instead of glum faces everyone was smiling. The number of events put on across the area grew considerably and overall there was a feeling that the community was coming together after years of attrition.

I began to see that even the smallest of changes could make a difference, and if one person became involved it usually followed that others would too; a kind of ripple effect spread across the entire community. It was my wish that communities took 'ownership' of their area, rather than waiting for agencies to do it for them. That was very evident in Offerton, where Hayley Bell, a mother of eight children, was constantly having to take her kids to different clubs. Not all ages fit into one specific club, of course. And so she decided to do something about it herself. She looked into community funding and, on the back of a successful application, set up a Mums' Group on the estate. This enabled hundreds of people to come together for a couple of fun-days organised by the group. From this, the group worked hard to establish itself in a premises and, after a lot of hard fighting, the old social club on the estate was reopened for its use. Although she was a mum of eight kids, one of whom had a chronic lung disease and needed a lot of nursing, Hayley was a tireless worker for the community and her efforts really paid off – anti-social behaviour on the estate went down by 40 per cent as the group gathered in strength. And Hayley found that as she galvanised support for a stronger community, that community started to help her. She described her experiences with the project in the report:

I have enjoyed the energy the Newlove project has created, all the services coming together responding to the call to action has been good. [. . .] Things are changing, Offerton is starting to get more connected. The only way we can be a strong, resilient community is if we are connected. We now need more individuals coming forward to support their community – that would make a huge difference.

In Merthyr Tydfil, the overriding problem was one very close to my heart – abuse of alcohol. Drunken teenagers, their senses dulled and inhibitions released through binge drinking, had murdered Garry as an evening's entertainment – even laughing about it later with mates. Merthyr Tydfil wasn't the easiest to get to and it seemed closed in on itself, a situation that I've often seen go hand-in-hand with under-age drinking and the problems that causes. People living in these places seem to give up and barricade themselves in against the anti-social behaviour that accompanies out-of-control public drinking. Jan Palmer is a community activist who is not ready to give up by any means. She is passionate about turning things round and improving the lives of everyone, particularly young people. Jan was keen to find a venue that could house a number of groups and activities, but time and again she was coming up against bureaucracy that seemed to be putting obstacles in her way. Nevertheless, she kept going, and I was determined that she shouldn't be put off by the form filling and the frustration of dealing with people who don't seem to understand you. I've had plenty of experience of this myself since Garry died and I always try to explain myself and my ideas in layman's terms.

Policy is very dry and if ordinary people can't interpret it, especially when they're applying for funding or requesting agency help, what use is it? Not being clear simply causes frustration at grassroots level, making people believe that the government (whoever that might be at the time) doesn't know, doesn't care or, worse still, does it deliberately to lock them out.

At all the places I visited, I shared my story, describing how a set of terrible circumstances forced an ordinary person like me to get up and do something. People can relate to that. They think that if one victim of anti-social behaviour can shout out against it, so can they. I understand what community activists are telling me, and it's a bugbear of mine that other people who are in positions of authority, as well as elected politicians, don't get out there and really listen to the people they claim to represent or work for. They are certainly paid by them through their taxes! They are not just there for election time. There is nothing more annoying when you are told how you must live in your backyard from a person or an organisation that doesn't live there.

Over the course of six months, I met many incredible people and was privileged to have shared their stories as well as my own. It was heart-warming to see just how strongly people felt about where they lived, especially in areas which had almost insurmountable problems, and how protective they were of one another. The funding we were able to provide was very useful, even though it wasn't huge, but the money isn't everything. Far more vital to a community's health is its spirit – the feeling that getting involved is worthwhile and beneficial – and it can lead to real change. That was my main motivation: to encourage people who might not have the confidence to get involved and show them that, however they participated, they could make a difference.

The conclusion of the 60-page report – 'Our Vision for Safe and Active Communities' – was a 12-point plan that I hoped would make the government realise there are ways of galvanising a community into action. I felt the points were easy to understand and highly deliverable. I've set them out below:

1 Reward communities who come together to reduce crime by giving them back money to re-invest in crime prevention.

2 Give the community cash from assets seized from drug dealers and other criminals.

3 Create a national information source, a hub for activists, and support it with an award for the best examples of activism.

4 Provide the public with a single point of contact for reporting non-emergency crime and anti-social behaviour – make sure other partners are linked up for the roll-out of the 101 number [the new number to call the police about non-life-threatening situations].

5 Let communities set their own speed limits.

6 Back a community 'Power of Competence' with a helpline to give the public advice to overcome cautious agencies standing in their way.

7 Follow the Neighbourhood Policing example and get the justice system out of the court room and into communities, and put victims' needs and their protection at the heart of any action.

8 Pool agencies' budgets locally and give the community a choice about how money is spent.

9 Ask Police and Crime Commissioners to commit at least 1% of their budget to grassroots community groups to use or have a say on them.

10 Take crime maps to the next stage – don't just show where crime happens, but what action has been taken against local crooks.

11 End the 9–5 culture. Agencies need to be there for their community when they need them.

12 Get public servants out and into communities, and volunteering their time and expertise to support local groups.

I will admit a couple of these were not issues I would have chosen, but I did compromise as I could live with them. You'll have to guess which ones they were! I wanted to put tackling alcohol abuse and anti-social behaviour on this list but it wasn't agreed. People who know me would have known it only made me more determined to do this, and I would have my chance when I moved over to the Department for Communities and Local Government. But more about that later.

The report was very well received in government circles and its recommendations were even discussed by the Cabinet. I then received a telephone call in my office at the House of Lords from Flo, who works for the Conservative Peers alongside the Leader of the House. I was amazed when she told me she'd heard that Conservative backbenchers in the Lords wanted to have a debate in the Chamber on my report. While I thought that was quite an accolade, there was just one problem – if this was to happen and I was to present the report to the House, I would obviously need to speak about it. But I hadn't yet made my maiden speech. I knew this was looming, but I'd kept putting it off. The truth is that I was extremely nervous about it. I felt I wasn't qualified enough to stand up in the House of Lords and share my thoughts in front of all these educated, titled people. Even though I'd spoken all over the place, there was something about debating in Parliament that made my stomach wobble with fear every time I thought about it. There it was again, the Hilda Ogden factor; the feeling that I'd wandered into Parliament by mistake and really shouldn't be there at all, coupled with my shyness and lack of confidence in my own personal qualities. I can talk and fight for England for the rights of the underdog – but not for me. Strange, I know, but that's me.

'Ah, that could be a problem,' I told Flo, and explained that I had not yet made my maiden speech.

Flo assured me it was no problem. She had already thought about how we would achieve this. There was to be a second reading of the Police Reform and Social Responsibility Bill on 27 April 2011, and she thought I could make my maiden speech during this debate. It would be an appropriate moment for me to get up on my feet and get it over with.

I spoke to Baroness Warsi and my mentor Baroness Morris about it, telling them how nervous I was and how I felt I was only here because I'd lost Garry. What could I possibly say that would make them sit up and listen to me?

'Don't be silly,' they replied. 'That's not true at all. Yes, you did lose Garry but you're here because you're you and what you've chosen to do since he died. You've got every right to be here.'

Well, their words got me thinking and I tried to look at the whole maiden-speech thing differently. If I wanted to make a difference and be the voice of ordinary people in the House, which I did, I had to do it. With Rani by my side, I drafted a few words that I hoped would explain who I was, why I was there and what I wanted to do. I poured my heart and soul into that speech, agonising over whether it would be too short or too long. Would I look as if I was going for a sympathy vote? Would it do justice for Garry and other victims? But also would it upset those I loved most – my parents and my girls?

We wrote and rewrote it until it was what I wanted it to be. Then we timed it with a stopwatch to check it didn't run over 11 minutes. I am a terrible fusspot, but at last I was satisfied. I didn't want them to be falling asleep, even though people say that they do that anyway. So I said they will have to like it or lump it. I only hoped there wasn't some centuries-old law that meant they could take away my peerage for making a rubbish speech. Then I waited anxiously as the days crept closer to D-Day at the House of Lords. And when the day finally arrived, oh boy, did I feel sick!

NINETEEN

Maiden Speech

Before I knew it, 27 April 2011 was upon me. I could hardly force down a mouthful of breakfast I was so anxious. There were 52 names on the speakers list that day, including my own, but at least I wasn't the only one making a maiden speech; Baroness Berridge and Lord Blencathra were perhaps feeling the same as I was that morning – both nervous and excited. I'd have been in a worse state had I known that my speech would be recorded for posterity so anyone can go on to the Parliament website and call it up, listen and watch. I was so green that I thought, if I made dog's dinner of it, only those in the Chamber would witness my humiliation, and with luck I'd get away with it!

The second reading of the Police Reform and Social Responsibility Bill began around 4 p.m. and, as with any debate, there are rules and respect to follow. If your name is down on the list, you have to be in from the time the minister opens the debate and stay until the end when the minister closes it. As in the Commons, members of the Lords can come in and out when people are speaking during a debate, but when a maiden speech is being made the doors are locked and no one is allowed to move until it's over. Of course, as someone on the maiden-speech list, I had to be there for the entire session. I was scheduled to stand up somewhere in the middle of the debate, so I realised that I wouldn't be out of the House before midnight. There was no going back now.

Baroness Berridge made her speech first and, as to be expected of a barrister, it was witty, polished and raised laughs and lots of approving nods. In it, she mentioned me, saying that, along with various other social campaigners she'd met, I was 'working to change things for the better'. I was delighted and honoured to have had a mention, but I wondered if people would make comparisons and whether I could meet her incredibly high public-speaking standards.

At 6.40 p.m., my turn came. With a pounding heart and a dry mouth, I stood up, the A4 pages of my speech shaking in my hands. 'Look after me, Garry,' I said silently, then started to speak.

My Lords,

I was amazed but apprehensive when the Prime Minister asked me to join you, and I feel truly humbled and honoured to be here today. I want so passionately to do justice for the many campaigners and victims whom I represent. I know that I am hugely privileged to be singled out, and I promise that I will give every ounce of my strength, every breath, so that I do not let them, your Lordships or the Prime Minister down. I wish to thank my sponsors, my noble friends Lord Strathclyde and Lady Warsi, and my wonderful, warm and kind mentor, my noble friend Lady Morris of Bolton. I thank especially all the employees of your Lordships' House: my friends the doorkeepers, the attendants and the wonderful staff and catering staff. They have shown me great kindness and respect. Their warmth has meant so much to me and they deserve their recognition for keeping the wheels turning smoothly here.

I might speak in simple words and not be as polished as many of your Lordships here today, but every word comes from my heart. There is such a wealth of experience, knowledge and humanity in this place. I look to your Lordships' House to help me, a novice, make this a safer and happier country. I cannot change the past but I will do all I can to improve the future.

I dedicate my speech to my late husband Garry and to my beautiful daughters for their courage and strength. Without their love and support, I would not have wanted to go on living. Together, the girls and I set up Newlove Warrington and we are working on establishing a youth zone based on the brilliant model of Bolton Lads & Girls Club to enrich the lives of young people. I also thank my elderly parents for their love, guidance, discipline and strong core values, which have shaped my life and which I try to pass on.

Last year, I became Government Champion for Active, Safer Communities, and I have met brave and inspiring citizens from all walks of life. These quiet, unsung heroes just get on making their neighbourhoods better places to live. They are good neighbours and they strengthen my belief in the better side of human nature, while exposing the darker element of suffering still out there, to our shame. My report, 'Our Vision for Safe and Active Communities', is their voice, and together we stand a real chance of rebuilding parts of our damaged society. I am also delighted to work within the Department for Communities and Local Government, and across Whitehall, to implement my report's recommendations, and I ask you to support them and me.

I am just an ordinary woman from a working-class background propelled into this elevated position by a set of horrifying circumstances, which I wish with all my heart had never happened. Almost four years ago, I was a wife, married to Garry for twenty-one years, and a mother of three children: Zoe, then

18, Danielle, 15, and Amy, only 12. Garry had been struck down with cancer at the age of 32 and had to have his whole stomach and spleen removed. Together, we fought and beat it as a loving, united family. Garry was brave, funny, the life and soul of the party, and he adored us, which makes all the more terrible the senseless way in which we lost him.

Our neighbourhood was bothered by groups of youths hanging around an underpass near to our home, drinking, swearing and being a nuisance. I attended neighbourhood meetings about them but it was treated as low-crime, anti-social behaviour, so not a priority. On the evening of 10 August 2007, Garry had gone out barefooted to investigate breaking glass outside our home. Our next-door neighbour was a young woman alone with a baby, and he was worried about their safety. Like a hunted animal, he was brought down by the baying, laughing gang whom he had questioned, in front of our horrified daughters. At one stage, there were more than 15 around him, boys and girls, aged between 14 and 18 years, high on drugs, alcohol and adrenalin. Within minutes, Garry suffered 14 ferocious kicks to the head as well as suffering 40 internal injuries. On 12 August, I woke up a wife but went to bed a widow.

Some of these teenagers had been in trouble with the law from only 11 years of age, and I ask: where were their feckless parents? Our girls watched their beloved father being murdered; they were covered in his blood. At the ten-week murder trial, they had to relive that experience minute by minute, to be cross-examined by five QC barristers. My 12-year-old daughter was told not to show emotion or fidget when being questioned via video link, but my girls bravely told the truth. They helped bring some of the guilty to justice.

There is so much in the criminal justice system that is so wrong. The victim or their families are given scraps from the table. That is why I am working with Victim Support, the national charity supporting all victims, as well as witnesses. For too long, victims have been second-class passengers, with the offenders and their needs in the driving seat. It is time that we were treated with respect and allowed to participate in the criminal justice system – and even allowed to take the driving wheel sometimes. If victims do not have confidence in the justice system, then we all suffer. If frightened witnesses will not give evidence, cases will collapse and offenders will walk away. That surely cannot be allowed to happen.

I also have to ask: why have we let our lovely towns and villages, so charming by day, turn into Dodge City at night, infested with drunken, brawling people, vomiting and causing chaos? They cost us billions of pounds, their violence immeasurable in lost innocent lives. They prevent ordinary people enjoying a night out. We must return to social drinking, get rid of under-age and binge drinking, and work closely with the drinks industry to educate and promote safe, sensible alcohol consumption. I will make that one of my top priorities.

Since that terrible night when Garry died, I have campaigned for victims whose lives are blighted by thugs. Minor crime, disorder and anti-social behaviour should be a huge warning bell to us all. Unless this behaviour is nipped in the bud, it grows like a cancer, unseen and undetected until it blooms like a malignant flower, which, as we know, can kill. Stories like the Pilkingtons' or the Askews', where isolated and vulnerable people have been bullied and hounded to death, are a disgrace and must not continue to happen. But I know that the big society is out there. It has been simmering for years on low heat with no name. Good neighbours and good deeds exist and we must learn from them. We must celebrate them and give them the resources and the power to turn up the heat. I believe we need that fuel of people power to make a difference. Cynics may knock it, but I know that it works. I stand before you to show that it can propel anyone to the greatest heights. Personal responsibility is the price we pay for all the good things that we take for granted. We have shelter, food, education, access to free worship and free speech, and many countless blessings. Children and young people have to be taught moral values and standards, and also that community, family and a love of our country are things to honour and cherish, not to mock and deride.

When we enter a period of peace and kindness in this country, when everyone is able to go about their lives safely, day or night, then, and only then, will Garry's legacy, the high price he paid with his life, be deemed by me to be almost worth the cost.

Phew! I sat down, pretty much out of breath and almost overcome with emotion, but to a rousing 'Hear, hear' from the Chamber. Up in the public gallery, Rani was in tears. I was told later she wasn't the only one. As I was speaking, I'd been aware that the House had fallen strangely silent. I'd hoped I wasn't boring them with my plain speaking, and I kept looking at the clock to make sure I kept to the time and didn't drone on.

I needn't have worried. The peers seemed pleased with what I'd just said and I heard the murmur of congratulations all around me. Then Baroness Meacher stood up and thanked me for 'an incredibly moving speech'.

'We have heard some very fine speeches today,' she said. 'My speech will be extremely quickly forgotten, but I will never forget that speech – it was amazing. Not only has the noble Baroness made a very important contribution today, but I have absolutely no doubt that she will be a very important contributor to the work of this House, representing very effectively the issues of victims and of the social problems in our communities. I cannot say more than to welcome her and thank her for joining us.'

Then she added, 'I feel like sitting down right now!'

Her words brought tears to my eyes. I was totally and utterly gobsmacked. All these highly educated successful people, listening, not just politely but intently, to what I had to say and appreciating it. They'd made me very welcome, and a bit closer to feeling 'part of the club'.

Silently, I thanked Garry for watching over me while I'd spoken. 'Did I do you proud, hon?' I asked silently. I prayed I had.

I was pleased that it was over and I could now get on with the business of being an active member of the House of Lords. But the impact of my speech seemed to be significant. I had so many handwritten messages of support, and anti-social behaviour began to be pushed higher up the national 'to-do list'. Here are a few comments:

Dear Helen,

I was so glad to have been in the chamber to hear your maiden speech. It was an enormously brave and impressive contribution, and obviously had a tremendous effect on everyone who was listening. So many congratulations and my very best wishes for your career in the Lords.

From The Rt Hon Baroness Hayman, Lord Speaker of the House of Lords

Dear Helen,

That was an amazing maiden speech. I don't suppose the chamber has seen anything like it before – and I wasn't the only one to wipe away a tear. Well done. Onwards . . .

Very best wishes

Anne, The Rt Hon Baroness Jenkin of Kennington

Dear Helen,

A belated note just to congratulate you on a very impressive maiden speech. Apart from being most moving, it was passionately presented . . . The fact that you could have heard a pin drop during your speech is testament to its impact and effectiveness.

Best regards

The Rt Hon The Viscount Younger of Leckie

I was swamped by invitations to national conferences but now I was being asked to be the keynote speaker (who, *me?*), and I often double-checked the envelopes to make sure they hadn't got into my cubby hole by mistake. It seemed unreal.

A few weeks before my maiden speech, and following another couple of meetings at Number 10, it was decided that I would move from the Home Office to the Department for Communities and Local Government, presided over by the formidable Eric Pickles.

I say 'formidable'. That's what I'd heard, anyway. 'Oh, he can be a bit of a bruiser . . .'; 'He doesn't suffer fools gladly . . .' that kind of thing. But I believe in making my own mind up about people, after I've met and talked with them.

When I met him, we hit it off straight away. He reminded me a bit of Fred Trueman, the Yorkshire cricketer who spoke his mind and was well liked for it. Eric told me that he wanted me to continue the role of Government Champion for Active, Safer Communities and extend the outreach work I'd done for my report into new areas. I would be working closely with the ministerial team in the department to develop policy that helped grassroots community activists, and report back to ministers about how to help such communities.

This didn't mean it was all plain sailing from then on but it certainly helped me steer things in the direction I wanted to go. I refused to let myself be blown off course any more.

I've publicly called Eric my rock – he has been as good as his word and his door is always open if I ever need him. And one of these 'little chats' resulted in my 'pot' of £1 million for community-led alcohol projects, so I was on top of the world.

I had been given the opportunity to work in a role about which I felt passionately and in which I knew I could make a real difference. I couldn't wait to get started, and in my mind I was already rolling up my sleeves for battle.

TWENTY

Building Safe, Active Communities

The announcement of my new role in the Department for Communities and Local Government was made on the same day as my maiden speech. This time I would be focusing on three areas that I thought would get things moving on the ground for activists. The first was the creation of a 'one-stop' website that would collate information, making it far easier for activists to find the information they needed. Time after time I'd heard the complaint that it was often difficult to locate relevant government information on the internet because it was all over the place, and more often than not written in the kind of language that would put off even the most educated people. The idea was to bring it all together in what was described as a 'barrier-busting' website, using language that ordinary people like me could understand. I did think it was a good idea – but it wasn't mine. I was learning to compromise with the civil-service machine and I was passionate about the next two priorities.

The second area of focus was a drive for volunteering among public sector workers. Civil servants, in particular, have a wealth of skills and experience, but, generally, they're so busy with paperwork they never have the chance to get out of the office and see what they can achieve on the ground. We wanted to encourage volunteering among this sector so that their valuable skills, such as IT, project management and dealing with complex bureaucracy, could be shared. I managed to hook up with an amazing charity called True Volunteer Foundation (TVF), who to this day continue to deliver this objective as well as support for my other projects at no cost. Because their volunteers generally come from the private sector, it's refreshing to see that they work faster and in a more joined-up way than the 'red-taped' and 'rules-bound' civil service. I hope they will be able to breathe fresh life, innovation and motivation into the officials they help to get out in the real world. Time will tell.

The third strand of this initiative was tackling under-age drinking. Interestingly, it was set as the last priority . . . However, I was happy to let the press release go out like that. I knew I would make it my top target, but I could wait – I was learning how to play the game! Naturally, this one was the closest to my heart and Eric thought I'd be the perfect person to get the various agencies and the drinks industry round the table to discuss ways of preventing under-age drinking and its associated problem of anti-social behaviour.

I was offered the chairman's role of a new advisory board, Community Alcohol Partnerships (CAP). (Everyone wanted my advice, it seemed, except my children who invariably ignored it!) The aim of CAP is to encourage both enforcement – in terms of police, trading standards and retailers working together to stamp out illegal sales and therefore under-age drinking – and education in schools, sixth-form colleges and youth centres on the dangers of alcohol abuse. Almost £1 million was put into the pot for the extension of CAP across the country as part of the trade's commitment to the Responsibility Deal by the alcohol industry linked to my appointment.

Some people might say, 'Why are you involving the drinks

industry? Surely that's part of the problem?' But I've never said we should ban alcohol. That would be ridiculous; it's part of our national culture and, besides, the alcohol industry employs a lot of people in the UK and their voices must be heard alongside those of others. Getting the drinks industry to monitor what it does, in terms of advertising, targeting of the young, and how and where alcohol is marketed and sold is a vital component to success, and CAP's work helps me deliver at least part of this agenda.

Getting round the table to discuss such issues really helps. You can't begin to understand how the drinks industry works until you hear it first-hand. Of course, I have to be very clear that I'm not available for lobbying on behalf of the drinks industry, and before I joined CAP I had to know what does and does not constitute lobbying. Certainly, the round-table approach does work. In 2009 – before I joined CAP, I should point out – Heineken ended production of its infamous White Lightning brand of strong, cheap cider thanks to pressure from campaigners. The company listened to the issues, understood what people were saying and took action. To me, that is a perfect example of what can be achieved when issues are aired in a sensible debate. For my own part, the past couple of years have seen me travelling across the UK to see CAP schemes in action, witnessing for myself how traders are working with police to combat under-age drinking and anti-social behaviour.

For example, I travelled to Great Yarmouth to launch a CAP-supported scheme. I looked at specific areas around the town centre and the seafront that suffered from alcohol abuse, and met the partnership, including local authority and police, who offered education about selling alcohol to young people and also about 'proxy buying' (i.e. adults buying booze for kids).

All well and good, but, as we've seen in the past, you can't go in waving a big stick. It turns people right off, especially teenagers, and makes everyone feel like criminals. Much better to use a carrot-and-stick approach and coax them into accepting better behaviour patterns, rather than me speaking psychobabble – there's a highly educated group of academics in Number 10 called the Nudge Group doing just that! So CAP donated £10,000 towards a naval cadet corps training scheme that aimed to give experience and hands-on learning to young people interested in a career in the maritime industry. The scheme was also aimed at diverting those young people away from a life hanging round the shops, drinking cheap strong booze and then causing trouble.

This CAP also works with the town's Salvation Army, which, for many decades, has tried to help those with alcohol problems, non-judgementally and often against the odds. In Great Yarmouth, the Salvation Army had set up a one-stop shop to offer advice and help to street drinkers and others in difficult situations. I really admire the work they do, and have done for so many years.

On 3 August 2012, I returned to the town to launch the *Newlove*, a training boat for cadets aged 8–18, which offers after-school training that could lead to employment in the local maritime industry. This diversionary project will keep young people from hanging around in crowds on street corners and parks, getting up to no good, and at risk of being tempted by under-age boozing. The CAP's £10,000 grant attracted funding from the local authority, trading standards and community safety partnership.

My first report didn't extend to Northern Ireland but it was read with interest there because they have a number of grassroots anti-social behaviour projects that dovetailed with my own. Besides, there is a CAP project in Derry that I was keen to see, so I was invited over to Belfast – my first visit to

Northern Ireland – to have a look around and see where we had common ground.

I really enjoyed my time in Northern Ireland, and found the people I met particularly warm and inspiring. Over the years, both the Catholic and Protestant communities have faced challenges that almost make the problems in English towns and cities pale by comparison but, as ever, there are bands of dedicated activists prepared to challenge the status quo and work to make their communities safer and more pleasant to live in, despite the violence that simmers just below the surface and sadly boils over now and then. Here I was treated like a real 'Lady'. My secretary Hari and I were put up in Hillsborough Castle, the Queen's palace when she visits. It was an amazing experience wandering around a real live castle that was put exclusively at my disposal. Another 'pinch me, am I dreaming?' moment in my life. Eh, Helen Newlove, who would have thought it? The only thing that brought us down to earth a bit was that the staff had gone home by the time we arrived after the press launch and evening reception. We hadn't time to share the community buffet provided so we ate our hastily purchased convenience-store sandwiches and tinned soup using gold-rimmed crockery and tipped our cans of soft drink into crystal goblets.

I was welcomed to Stormont by Peter Robinson, the Northern Irish Assembly's First Minister, where the reception I mentioned was held for the 'Street By Street' project, located in East Belfast. This was a partnership between local groups and the Police Service of Northern Ireland, and involved community workers taking to the streets every Friday and Saturday nights, looking out for anti-social behaviour and other problems. I also went to Derry to see the people from the CAP project who work around some of the really tough estates there. I was told that a lot of kids gather on those streets at weekends, so the activists really have their work cut out. One woman told me that one evening she challenged a drunk young girl, asking why she drank the way she did and then went on to give her sexual favours to anyone who asked.

'Dunno,' came the reply. 'Just what you have to do today, innit?'

'OK, then,' said the woman. 'How much money have you got on you?'

The girl looked puzzled. 'About £2,' she replied.

'Right, hand it over,' the activist said, putting out her hand.

The girl looked puzzled and annoyed. Why should she do that?

'So you're more protective over that two quid than you are over your own body?' the activist said. 'You'll look after your money but you won't look after your health?'

I thought that was a very clever way of challenging a young person like her, and it was obviously doing some good because statistics showed that alcohol-related incidents were down by 50 per cent in some areas – an amazing achievement. Please read my report for more – there are so many examples of people working away in silos and it is very frustrating when they don't learn from one another and share their knowledge. So it really gives me a glow to see informal partnerships developing when I speak. My two areas – East Belfast and Derry – are visiting each other and working together, which is what it is all about, isn't it? Not exactly rocket science.

My passion to tackle the anti-social behaviour related to binge and under-age drinking still burns brightly. Although it does not take a lot of money to make big changes, it can make a difference. (East Belfast CAP – called CUD – did it with a £500 donation to make a DVD on their success, which they show at meetings. Resources were there within their community. All it took was a partnership group to pinpoint where to direct it.) I wanted to show that the principles of CAP – getting everyone around the table to come up with a common plan of action – could drive down anti-social behaviour significantly. I could show the huge improvements to the Newlove Neighbourhoods with their small £15k grants.

Money was tight and budgets had been slashed everywhere. But I needn't have worried. It did take time getting it through the system but, finally, in early 2012 it was announced that £1 million would be given to ten communities that had made successful applications to the government's 'Alcohol Fund', set up to help grassroots projects tackle problem drinking. I was learning and took control of this from the start. I whittled down a huge application form that would have put off most normal people, wrote to all the chief constables asking them to gee up their ground troops to get good community projects to apply and saw the leader of the Local Government Association to advertise the scheme. I even did a video clip urging activists like me to look at it and try not to think it wasn't for them.

The areas – Bury, Chelmsford, Cornwall, County Durham, Lincoln, Maidstone, Moseley, Newcastle, Shropshire and Wakefield – were chosen after a difficult selection process that saw applications oversubscribed ten times over, which says an awful lot about the problems of alcohol abuse on our streets.

Each community has its own particular difficulties. For example, Shropshire's project will look at five of the county's public parks that experience seasonal summertime issues around under-age drinking and anti-social behaviour, while Moseley in Birmingham wants to establish a permanent solution to street drinking and problems of begging, littering and rough sleeping. As I write, we are touring these communities to see what progress has been made, and how we can encourage new initiatives and grassroots activists to keep up their good work.

All this came off the back of my third report, 'Building Safe,

Active Communities: Strong Foundations by Local People',
published in February 2012. The report set out progress on
the three priorities I've mentioned. It also updated the 12
challenges to action around anti-social behaviour and alcohol
that I outlined in my first report. The new report came hard
on the heels of the summer 2011 riots – an incredibly shocking
and destructive outburst of mass anti-social behaviour which
I felt was totally unjustified especially when – as usual – it was
innocent people such as shopkeepers and bystanders who
suffered from all the violence and looting. This is what I had
to say about it in my introduction to the report:

On four terrible days last summer the world was appalled by
scenes of group madness, criminality and callous uncaring
vandalism. Riots exploded on the streets of towns and cities
around England, testing our police and emergency services to
the limit. Maurice Reeves stood heartbroken in the ashes of his
family's Croydon furniture store that had withstood two World
Wars, only to be reduced to a blackened ruin by the mindless
action of a few.

But it is not just during the riots that we are threatened by
people who feel so disengaged from normal rules of behaviour
that they think they can take what they want – and to hell with
the consequences. They may be a minority, but they take a lot
of our attention and money – it sometimes feels as though the
99% of good kids are ignored while we focus dwindling resources
on the 1% who go astray. But we can do something about this.
Children and teenagers need rules to live their lives, and
opportunities to mix socially in safety so they become good
citizens, and maximise their potential.

I am sick of the harm caused by a rising tide of people who
put themselves and others at risk from illegal and irresponsible
drinking. I will make tackling 'Binge Britain' my central aim

for my next year's work. The efforts so far to get to grips with this problem have not been effective enough. I'm personally committed to see through a raft of measures nationally that will tackle the alcohol abuse that drags places down, spreading fear and anxiety in communities in place of satisfaction and pride. And I'll bring everybody to the table – politicians, police, traders, manufacturers and retailers, educationalists and health professionals, as well as charities and agencies – to do so.

I want to see a culture of responsible drinking so we can rid our streets of drunken violence and intimidation. I want children and parents to understand the terrible, long-term damage to health from alcohol abuse. We can achieve this through education and I want to see far more joined up and effective working by agencies to tackle this together. I am delighted people in communities around the country, like in Newquay and Northern Ireland, found ways to combat this problem. We need to harness their ideas and their spirit of innovation.

We need to resurrect that fighting spirit that we are so good at generating when our backs are against the wall. We've always pulled together in times of great national need and my report sheds light on the work of many people who are doing just that. We need to support and encourage them, not hold them back, spreading their good practice and celebrating their successes. There are projects which have been proven to work. Those behind them want them rolled out nationally. But they often meet with frustration and many blocks and bureaucratic hurdles, and the years pass as they face demands for more reports, evaluations and 'expert' advice before anything can be agreed.

I also reported on the creation of the 'Newlove Neighbourhood Programme', a series of one-stop shops launched by the True Volunteer Foundation to help local activists to be more effective in their approach to raising funding and promoting local activities within their communities. TVF offered a non-ring-fenced donation from a private donor of £1,000 each to every one of the seven neighbourhoods I worked with around the time of my first report. As I said, 'By removing the burden of red tape and trusting the activists to spend it on ways to build community resilience, this has been a boost to these local people struggling to find money to make their plans a reality.'

Jan Palmer, the community volunteer from Merthyr Tydfil, described the challenges the community group faced and how they overcame them:

> The extra £1,000 from the charity TVF was a big bonus as it came without strings for us to decide what we wanted to do with it.
>
> We have finally opened our youth club and it is going really well. We open three days a week and have tried to include all ages. We do two nights for eleven to eighteen year olds and one for the younger children. Also, the mother and toddler group opens two mornings a week for birth to five year olds. The parents help to run that and are showing great community spirit.
>
> I have arranged for all volunteers to be trained. I now have five qualified level two youth workers and one level three. I have got another three going on a level three course on Monday that I organised myself. I have put them through child protection courses and first aid. I did ask all the partnerships for help with getting application forms for funding for rent, but I did that myself also by downloading from the internet.
>
> I am also in the process of applying to have our own youth centre built with another group in the area with Councillor Jones.
>
> Anti-social behaviour is very low and the under age drinking

seems to have stopped. We get very few problems now, as I have worked very hard with the police to reduce this. Together we seem to be winning but it's early days yet.

The road safety people and the fire service come and speak to the kids about fire and being safe on the roads. We had a great Christmas party with one of our PCSOs as Santa. The police have been very supportive and help out a lot. They often call in and have a game of pool with the kids and they seem to have a great relationship with them.

We have lots of things planned for the coming months with a street party in the park for the Queen, carnival and days out for the kids.

The Baroness has made me realise that I am capable, and so are my helpers. We don't have to rely on 'agencies' doing it for us all the time. If we are shown how, we can run things the way we want them, not how others think it should be.

As well as helping to build better and safer communities across Britain, the other strand of my work in Parliament is as a voice for victims and witnesses. This was an area in which I wanted to work right from the start. Child bereavement is a specialist area that is very limited. Months before the trial, we were offered support from the NSPCC for Amy, which the police had a struggle themselves to find for us. They'd arranged for someone to come and see her before the trial started, as she was understandably nervous about the whole thing, and, of course, she was still only 12. Amy didn't really want to see anyone – she just wanted her dad back – but I begged and begged because I thought it would do some good, and finally she agreed to see a counsellor. Unfortunately, the counsellor didn't help the situation. She began to explain that in a court trial defendants are innocent until proven guilty, which is correct, but it doesn't really comfort a 12 year old who's lost her dad and hoping the bad people would be locked away so they couldn't hurt anyone else.

She also said she didn't know a huge amount about the case and that she had to remain strictly neutral. We were informed that Amy could visit a therapy room in Warrington, where there were paints and paper and she could express how she felt using those. After the woman left, I rang and complained, not so much about the individual, who was only doing her job according to the rules, but about a system which could treat a 12-year-old child so impersonally. The treatment we got as a family at Chester Crown Court, while well meaning, wasn't adequate either for the seriousness of the case or for the fact that some of us were witnesses. The scales are definitely not balanced.

When I came into the Lords, I met Javed Khan, who had just been appointed the chief executive of Victim Support. We were both new to our roles and, having spent time discussing victims and witnesses, we realised we shared some common ground. I admired his get-up-and-go, particularly where the victims of anti-social behaviour are concerned.

This meeting, and others like it, led to the setting up of the All-Party Parliamentary Group (APPG) for Victims and Witnesses of Crime, which I co-chair along with Rob Flello, the Labour Shadow Justice Minister. Victim Support was chosen as the APPG's administrator with the understanding that it is a platform for all groups and individuals in Parliament concerned with the rights of victims and witnesses. The group aims to build a broad coalition of support for discussion and policy outcomes and, to this end, we've invited various speakers and campaigning organisations to come along and raise awareness of the issues. We had a visit from Lord Woolf, the former Master of the Rolls and Lord Chief Justice of England and Wales, who pointed out that victims who refused to act as victims and had spoken out in support of their rights had made many definite changes to the way they are treated. It was good to hear that from one of the country's top judges.

Rob and I marked our first year in March 2012 with a joint decision to focus on selected topics close to victims' hearts, such as offender management, probation and release, access to court papers and victim statements. We want to produce a report which we will put to both Houses and hope it will stimulate debate and changes in law. It's a big job and will not be easy, as this is a highly emotional arena with many differing ideas and proposals from victims. I have met with the Justice Secretary, ministers and officials to ensure the pledge of 'putting victims at the heart of the criminal justice system' comes to life. I've spoken up in debates in the House and at conferences. Privately, I see families who write to me and I act as an advocate on their behalf where I can.

The election of Police and Crime Commissioners (PCCs), which took place in November 2012, raised a lot of concerns, and I disliked the politicising of issues around it. The public just didn't warm to the possibilities and the voter turnout was disappointingly low. PCCs will have access to resources that they can direct for services in their own areas. And for the first time they, and the police, will be accountable to the ordinary person in the street. My main concern has always been that everyone, including the PCCs, should be aware of their responsibilities to victims, and the APPG hopes to commission a survey of all areas to present to the new PCCs. I continue to speak at senior police conferences and also to ministers regularly behind the scenes.

I always argue for the fact that victims must be given greater respect in court. It seems to me that it is a basic right that victims should have a room to themselves for the duration of a court trial, and to be told what is happening at every stage.

Also, I think the public gallery should be separated so that victims and defendants' families and supporters are not all thrown together. It's an appalling situation and one that no victim should have to endure, sometimes for weeks on end. The same goes for juvenile witnesses. If the presumption is 'innocent until proven guilty' for defendants, why shouldn't the same apply to witnesses? My girls were grilled by the defence team until they were made to feel they were the guilty ones. What kind of situation is that? If we're talking about justice and fairness, then that balance should extend to victims and witnesses, otherwise it makes a mockery of the justice system. During the trial, there was a lot of talk about defendants' rights, but nothing about those of victims and witnesses. That's because they barely exist, and it is a situation that needs to be corrected. Just recently, I spoke to a woman whose husband died in a road-traffic incident and who was waiting for the court case to begin. Someone was accused of causing her husband's death, but because it was traffic related she wasn't treated as a victim should be. In the end, she had to beg her MP for contact from Victim Support. In another case, a family whose loved one was killed by a 4x4 while out cycling were treated just as badly. Just because there is some element of 'accident' involved doesn't mean to say that those left behind aren't victims. They are, and their rights should be acknowledged along with everyone else's.

In addition, it should also be recognised that it's not only offenders who go through the parole procedure. This will be something the girls and I will have to face in a few years' time and, having spoken to those families going through the same procedure, I realise it will not be pleasant. All they hear is: 'Well, they've done their time,' and, while that might be true, 'doing time' is something victims are never released from. I think, if we're going to have parole, the views of offenders and victims should be treated equally. I've heard stories about victims and their families hearing about parole-board meetings only a few days before they actually happen – hardly any time to prepare for something that big. Again, the justice system feels offender-led, and I think that is wrong.

The eventual release of prisoners is also cause for concern. We know they have to come out, even if we don't like it, but what we don't want is for the ex-prisoner to end up living around the corner. We know this happens on a regular basis, and it does nothing to help victims and their families rebuild their lives. No one wants to look at it from the victims' point of view. Through the *Dispatches* programme, I met a woman whose husband was attacked by thugs and left in a persistent vegetative state. She has two young sons and understandably has found it hard to move on with her life. The people convicted of her husband's attack are now out of prison and living nearby. Think for a moment how that must feel, and then tell me that criminals should have the right to live anywhere they choose.

Going through the process sounds all well and good, receiving manuals and leaflets in the post to say this is the next step, etc. However, let's strip it right back and see what really happens for victims. In all of this, a human being has been lost, never again to appear. How much weight does that fact really carry? It should be considered equally important as the rehabilitation of the offender. It sounds cheesy and people hear it all the time, but the 'life sentence' really is served by the victim's family, the damage irreparable. If we say too much, we are just angry people and want revenge. I always say, 'Stand in our shoes and say that to us.' The pain we suffer we cannot put into words and no one wants someone else to suffer as we do. I wouldn't wish it on my worst enemy. Much as I'd like to, I can't live anywhere near my late husband, because he's dead. For his sake, and for every other victim of crime in this country, I will make my voice heard loudly in Parliament.

As you might imagine, I get a lot of letters about anti-social behaviour, many of them written in desperation at the fact that nothing has been done to alleviate their problems. They say they're afraid of going outside and they believe that the police don't take them seriously. They say nothing will ever change, and that they've been forgotten by politicians. It's very sad indeed to think that so many people are struggling, and have been virtually imprisoned in their own homes by drunken louts. I know I'm only one cog in the machine but I do pass on letters to chief constables in the hope they will take notice and address problems on their patch. If I keep doing that, I hope I will have some impact. Garry's murder changed the way anti-social behaviour is dealt with and the more progressive police forces now look at it as a crime rather than a nuisance. So the language used in relation to anti-social behaviour is changing and that can only be a good thing. When defendants are no longer laughing in the dock and victims have the same rights as those who made them into victims, I feel my efforts will have achieved something.

There is definitely a moral backbone in this country, but it's one that people seem afraid to show for whatever reason. People know right from wrong; however, getting involved in that debate, and doing something about those wrongs, seems to make them suddenly shy. But, as I mentioned in my last report, it was inspiring to see what people did after the 2011 riots. Hackney is one of my neighbourhoods and, following the violence and looting, I went to a community meeting there. Community leaders earlier had gathered around 400 people at a local church with the intention of cleaning up the damage and it must have been amazing to see them march off to put their neighbourhood back together. The day after, young people handed out single white roses to passers-by to apologise for others and say they were not involved. That is backbone, that is taking back your streets and it flies in the face of the sorts of people who say, 'Oh, it's Hackney, what do you expect?' The community spirit witnessed there for days after the riots proved all those cynics wrong. People in deprived areas are as community-minded as people in wealthier places, if not more so, and to me they're an inspiration. I hope to work with such people for many, many years to come.

TWENTY-ONE

The Next Chapter

I'm aware that, with all the excitement of being elevated to the House of Lords and the intensity of my workload ever since, it might look as though I have forgotten my three daughters. Not so – Zoe, Danielle and Amy remain at the heart of everything I do, and, whenever I feel I've made some progress in the fight against anti-social behaviour or for the rights of victims and witnesses, I know I've done it for them.

We were always a close family and we remain so, despite what happened on that night in August 2007 that changed all our lives. My memories of that night are still a blur; the girls, however, had to keep their memories of their father's murder pin sharp in order to be credible witnesses in court. That they managed to keep their heads in the most horrible of circumstances, and later take the stand in court to face aggressive questioning, makes them all heroines in my eyes. Their bravery is beyond question – Zoe often says that the gang could've turned on Amy and beaten her to a pulp too, and then I would have had to say goodbye to two members of my family. They were all incredibly strong that night. Zoe was struggling to stop me seeing Garry lying on the ground, his face a bloody mess. Quite honestly, I was the child screaming and she was the adult.

And yet, apart from the mood swings and emotions – at times very angry ones – none of them has gone off the rails. Mind you, if they did and people said to me, 'Well, it's only to be expected,' I would say, and have said, 'No, losing their father is no excuse at all. They are being brought up with the same morals, values and respectful manners that Garry instilled in them while they were young. Their mum may be their only parent left and that is how they will carry on. Anything else would be disrespectful to their father's wishes.'

Amy once let rip at me over something trivial two years ago, and all the anger and pain that she'd kept to herself came spilling out of her. She says that it felt like another Amy had taken over her body and was aiming directly at me. At the heart of it, she just wanted her dad back – let's be truthful, her childhood had been taken away from her at 12 – and I could fully understand that. Afterwards, she felt better, and I wondered whether it might be a good time for her to examine her feelings more closely with a counsellor. She did go along but, true to form, she came back after one session and said it wasn't for her. Her mum and her sisters were the only ones she wanted to talk to, she said. Zoe thought Amy should go for a few sessions so that she could be properly assessed, but she didn't want to and we all had to respect that. She was determined to go back to school and face up to the stares and whispers that would inevitably follow her around, and she did it with positivity and the dry sense of humour she inherited from her dad.

Zoe and Danielle were knocked off their stride, academically, by Garry's death. They were heading for university and college respectively, but those dreams were ended, or at least postponed, by what happened. But they're both doing well and I'm proud that every day they get up and want to go out to work. Danielle loves photography and has a good eye for it, although at the moment she is working as a nursery nurse, which she loves. Jobs are very few and far between and so hopefully she will make her dream come true one day. Zoe is a successful make-up artist who is working hard to establish herself in a highly competitive industry. My baby of the family – Amy – wants to be the first Newlove to get to university, and I hope and pray that she achieves this. I'm sure she will.

Don't get me wrong – they still squabble when they're together and there can be pouting and pulled faces. But they're also incredibly protective of one another and if someone attacked one of them – verbally or otherwise – you would certainly see the fur flying. Perhaps that's just siblings for you, but they have huddled together noticeably since Garry's death.

Naturally, I see a lot of their father in them all, not least their height and their stubbornness. Mind you, they could have a double dose of that, as I'm no pushover. Garry used to call me 'vision with no sound' when we'd had an argument and I see the same in the girls. They all love music, which is definitely something they've inherited from their dad, and of course they're respectful of others and will stand up for the underdog. Zoe jokes that she's inherited their dad's compulsion for keeping things neat and tidy. She definitely has Garry's entrepreneurial streak and his vision for creating a better situation for himself and his family. She's a great one for blogging and isn't afraid to share her opinions with the world – OK, I think we know who she gets that from!

I truly want them to enjoy the rest of their lives and be happy in whatever they do. They have been scarred badly but they are strong women and, while they'll never be able to put the events of that night behind them, I hope they will learn to live with what happened and turn negatives into positives. They are doing that now, and I think it bodes very well for their futures. Of course, I worry about them as they grow older and

I hope they will have partners who will understand what they've been through and be supportive of them. I also wonder about children – part of me thinks they shouldn't have any because the world those newborns would come into isn't a particularly pleasant one, not at the moment anyway. But I am doing what I can to make the world a better place for any grandchildren I might have, and I know that thousands of others across the country are doing the same. Having grandchildren will be a strange experience; like everything else, I won't have Garry around to share in the pleasure they bring. That makes me sad, as does the fact that I can't share with him all the little joys the girls bring. But none of us wants to go back to what we call 'Day One'. It is hard, and there are days I'm tired of it all and I feel the struggle isn't worthwhile. But I know in my heart that it is, and that we have to go forward.

What happens when Swellings, Sorton and Cunliffe eventually come out of prison? I feel that will be the time I need to look for increased security both for myself and my girls. I'm preparing myself to be as strong as I can, but if I worried over it too much I would never go out again. Then they will have destroyed my life completely and I'll never allow them to do that. Nor do I want to meet those three. We talk about restorative justice for low-level crime, which I believe can work and I have seen for myself families coming together for the better in their communities. I also know that there are families who have met those convicted of crimes against them or their loved ones, and if that has helped with closure, then fine. It is up to the individuals and families to decide what is best for them, not the system or other people's opinions. But I can say that it's not a path I've chosen to go down. I realise that, in the work that I do, some day someone will ask me why I've made that decision. So what would my answer be? The reason is that those three never showed a shred of remorse in court and I don't believe they're remorseful now. They kicked Garry as he lay on the ground, without mercy, and they all pointed fingers at one another in court in order to excuse themselves. They couldn't take responsibility for their actions, and that's what sickens me the most. They had the opportunity to say sorry, but they didn't take it. Whatever words they could say to me now would be hollow and meaningless. The girls feel the same way; even more strongly, perhaps, because they saw exactly what happened. They believe the three should be kept in jail for the rest of their lives. I can't forgive the senseless way they killed Garry, and I never will.

I'm aware that Jordan Cunliffe's mum is campaigning for his release and, although I've been asked, I will never share a platform with her. I understand that she's his mum and she feels loyal to him. But I think it's disgraceful that she's campaigning for his release and she says she's fighting an unjust system. At the end of the day, she still has her son. One day he will come out and they will be reunited. In the meantime, she can go to visit him. All that the girls and I can visit is an urn.

Panorama made a programme about the law of joint enterprise, which called into question the safety of Cunliffe's conviction. They put my side, along with that of Mrs Cunliffe, and ideally they would have loved to interview us together in some kind of debate. I told them on camera that I believe that if you stand there and watch a person being kicked in the head and you do nothing, you're as guilty as the person doing the kicking. I was only on screen for a short while as I'd obviously not said what they wanted me to say. When journalists say they are neutral, I reply, 'How would you feel if your wife or husband had been beaten to a pulp?' I don't believe in neutrality over something as serious as this. You're either with me or against me.

Cunliffe appealed in the summer of 2010. As usual, I had to walk past an offender's family in order to enter the courtroom. His barrister told the three judges that his previous convictions should have been aired before the jury, because they didn't include any crimes of violence. But the judges rejected this, saying, 'We take the view that there is no basis upon which it can be said that it might have affected the verdict.

'In order to have the matter presented to the jury, the jury would have had to be told of those four previous incidents, wholly different in type, but nonetheless showing that this was a young man who had been in trouble with the law before.'

The judges said there was nothing that cast doubt on the safety of the murder conviction, and his appeal was rejected within an hour of his case being presented. Which I think says plenty about this young man's involvement in the death of my husband.

As for me, well, it's been a journey. That sounds like the biggest understatement of all time, but it's true. I'm not very good at dealing with my own problems – a bit like an accountant who gets someone else to do his own figures. I prefer going out into the world and seeing what I can help with on a wider scale. When people say 'thank you' for whatever we've managed to achieve, I feel embarrassed. I don't want to feel full of myself. All I've done is bring a bit of plain speaking into the mix, and hope that I've made a difference. I'm not Mother Teresa by any means. I'm Helen Newlove, and I'd rather people called me by my first name than anything else. Like everyone, I want a better life for my girls and I guess I'm like many proud but concerned mums in that respect.

I like working with young people and I enjoy being part of the Peers in Schools outreach programme that helps school- and college-age students understand more about Parliament and the House of Lords. The young people always want to know my story and I find they're very respectful when they listen to it. I don't want to bring these happy young people down; I just want them to know that they don't have the right to do what Swellings, Sorton and Cunliffe did when they were drunk and out of control. I tell them that there are other things in life besides drinking to excess. Some young people have a hard life, I know, but we're all free to change that if we really want to. That's what I try to tell them – that their future is in their hands, and their hands alone. In other words, think about what you're doing in all situations, and how your behaviour is impacting on others. I've met so-called gang members and I'm not intimidated by them. Again, I tell them what happened to me and they tend to go quiet. They're not all bad lads and girls, and sometimes they're unfairly labelled as 'gang members'. When we were young, we went round in a group but we weren't called a 'gang'. We were just a crowd of friends. I meet young people who associate with gangs and they've often got a terrible chip on their shoulders. 'Turn it into a positive,' I tell them. 'Don't go round for ever thinking the world is your enemy. Do something about it if you feel that way.'

That goes for everyone, not just young people. If you really want to make a change, don't rely on everyone else to do it for you. Go out and make it happen yourself. We live in a very individualistic culture – the attitude of 'What's in it for me?' is prevalent now. There is a lot of cynicism around too, but if I ever have such cynicism directed at me, I always reply, 'Well, what are you doing about it?' The answer is usually a blank stare, which means they're not doing a lot. When I speak I'm talking about real life, not abstract or theoretical situations, and I hope that by doing that people will take what I'm saying seriously. I've been called a mad and angry woman but what I actually am is a woman sickened by society's acceptance of desensitisation to what doesn't affect us. I have every right to be angry, but I'm conscious that we as victims shouldn't become bitter and that we restore our faith in society by doing good works on behalf of others. The girls are keen to be involved in the work I do and when the time is right I will let them. For now, I just hope that I've inspired people with my story, and that I make my family proud of what I am trying to do for them, and above all I hope that the work I've done, and continue to do, will keep Garry's memory alive and that his generosity of spirit and appetite for life will be an inspiration to me and my girls for as long as we all live. Believe me, it is not a cheesy strap line when you hear the families of victims of homicide say, 'We don't want anyone else to become a victim and suffer such pain.' This arena needs to be closed, not filled with more heartbroken individuals and families. I said at the beginning of this journey that I would make sure Garry would never be just another 'statistic' and that will always be my mantra.

Postscript

The Diamond Jubilee year of 2012 was one full of laughter and happiness for many. Just one year after the terrible city riots, London showed its friendly, happy face, put its best foot forward and joined the whole country in throwing open its arms in the biggest love-in ever seen in living memory. The world came to celebrate the best ever Olympics and we banished forever the old notion that Brits are all stiff upper lip and po faces. Her Majesty was showered with the respect and love of our nation and little children sang and waved flags, even in pouring rain. Much of this was achieved by the volunteers who came out in their thousands and shamed the cynics who said it would be a flop, that riots would return to our streets and that the Big Society is dead. A royal baby heralds more national joy for 2013.

As for my girls, Zoe is now 23, Danielle 20 and Amy reached a milestone 18. All are getting on with life, finding their own paths. It has been a very long and lonely road for me to walk alone since that night in 2007 when Garry was taken and our family ripped apart. I was resigned to the thought that my life would be my campaigning. I could look forward to seeing the girls settle with their own life partners, marry and have children. But I never thought that I would find another love like Garry.

But the best-laid plans, as they say . . .

I met Paul, a lovely man who became my friend, who taught me to laugh again. I was so shy and unable to reach out. I protected myself from further loss and hurt by living in a bubble. But this man was patient, kind and understanding. He realises the need within me to do what I can to make a difference. He is generous and big-hearted enough not to feel threatened or jealous of my work. And he is my number-one supporter.

Our family and friends watched the quiet blossoming of our relationship with mixed emotions, mostly hope that it would end in smiles not tears. In July 2012, in front of those who love us most, quietly and with little fuss, we became man and wife. Zoe was my matron of honour and Danielle and Amy were my bridesmaids.

Paul is a Scouser, so he and my mum get on famously. He has nothing to do with politics. He's content to stay out of the public eye and we want to live as normal a life as possible. When the news broke in the media, I was overwhelmed by the messages of support from the public. They wished us well and expressed their delight.

Sadly, just before Christmas 2012 and five months after we married, Paul's father Alan died of a massive heart attack. He was a wonderful, kind, loving man, always smiling, and I will miss him very much. So we have personal challenges in front of us as a couple with our remaining elderly parents who are in poor health to care for.

Professionally, I heard the news I was longing for only a short time after Paul's father passed away. I only wish he could have known what was to happen. I was appointed the new Victims' Commissioner after an open recruitment exercise to ensure victims' and witnesses' voices are brought to the heart of Government – doing what I have done for years, only this time with real clout. To obtain this non-governmental public appointment I had to be interviewed by a panel in the autumn of 2012. The role is to promote the interests of victims and witnesses, encourage good practice in their treatment and regularly review the Code of Practice for Victims.

I know about victims – I am one and I've been there. I know how it is when you feel the scales of justice are not balanced in your favour, even through you are the one suffering. I know how it feels when your grieving relatives are placed in the dock and forced to undergo cross-examination often far tougher than the defendant experiences. I understand the pain of the appeals procedure and the agony of parole boards. So I feel very qualified to take on this role, particularly having three years' experience of Westminster and Whitehall.

Presently, the status of victims is patchy. I'm pleased that we are now at least talking about victims, but there are still many people out there who have become victims and don't know where to turn. I don't intend to use sticking plasters in my new role; it will be my aim to make sure each and every victim is helped and supported in a way that shows them respect and understanding.

I am humbled yet immensely proud of this opportunity, and I welcome it as a chance to roll up my sleeves and get stuck in. It is a fitting end to this chapter of my life, while being the beginning of the next.

Life has the ability to surprise and amaze us when we are not looking. I can't predict what the future holds for me and my loved ones. But I am finishing this book as 2012 begins to fade and 2013 brings the promise of a new year, new challenges and new successes. I have tried to make the book a faithful record of the life of a funny, happy father and husband and how his tragic murder impacted my life and those who loved him, but also how its ripples spread on and on. That will be Garry's true legacy.

Rest In Peace, Garry Newlove; gone but never ever forgotten.